SomewhereBetween
EZEKIEL AND
MISS HAVISHAM

365 DAYS AT
THE CEMETERY

MARIANNE M JENNINGS

ISBN: 061558330X
ISBN 13: 9780615583303

To Claire, my teacher

TABLE OF CONTENTS

INTRODUCTION

My mother died on January 8, 2006. My youngest daughter died on January 11, 2007. I had just finished the challenging first year of grieving for my mother when my husband and I lost one of our children. That phrase sounds odd, as if we misplaced a child during a Universal Studios tour. Claire Elizabeth leaving us so soon after my mother's passing found me lost. Varnished platitudes about grief abound; the unvarnished truth about the challenges of grief is difficult to find. None of us will escape two things in this life: death and grief. Yet for all their universality, there's a dearth of helpful insights and guidance on the inescapable experience of grief. Oh, sure, there are health books a'plenty to help with the continuation of living, i.e., postponing death, each with a different remedy or niche cure: "Eat a rutabaga every day and you'll live to be ninety." But is a life filled with rutabagas worth living?

Grief remains an odd subject because the stories of how folks cope with it seem to be at 180-degree odds—extremists abound. You have Ezekiel, who hardly missed a beat, "So I spake unto the people in the morning; and at even my wife died; and I did in the morning as I was commanded" (Ezekiel 24:15). Ezekiel wasn't around for much of the illness and was pretty much ready to go the next morning. Lou Costello, one-half of the brilliant Abbott and Costello comedy team, was the same way. On November 4, 1943, he was returning to his radio show for the first time in six months following his recovery from rheumatic fever. When he arrived at the NBC radio studios, he was told that his son, Lou Jr., who was just two days away from his first birthday, had accidentally drowned in their swimming pool. Mr. Costello had wanted his young son to hear him on the radio that night. He did not cancel the broadcast but carried on without telling the audience what had happened. His only cryptic reference came through one line in the broadcast, "Wherever he is tonight, I want him to hear me." He had lost his son, but he still delivered laughs.

At the other extreme there is Miss Havisham of *Great Expectations,* who lost a love and then spent twenty-five years in a wedding dress with stopped clocks in dilapidated Satis House. Compeyson only left her standing alone at the altar, but she grieved for the remainder of her days. I was somewhere between Costello's and Ezekiel's get-up-and-go and Miss Havisham's frozen-in-time, one-outfit life. I was more like Woodrow Wilson because I felt my losses acutely. Mr. Wilson wrote, when his wife Ellen died in 1914, "I never dreamed such loneliness and desolation of heart possible."[2] Or maybe there was more C. S. Lewis in me. He spent one year writing about grief after his wife died.

I felt a bit embarrassed that I was experiencing such grief, for ours is a faith and a church with happy funerals. There is laughter at the service and even more at the luncheons afterward. We seem to be blessed with our share of Ezekiels. A widow in our ward stood the day after her husband's funeral and, without a tear, thanked us and offered her testimony of the gospel. I was in awe of her faith and strength but not possessed of either following my daughter's death. Many of the lessons in the Doctrine and Covenants course of study offer examples of the stalwarts in our church's history who carried on faithfully and joyfully after crossing the plains and losing *all* of their children. Who was I to complain? But, as a *Time* magazine writer once explained, "Grief is a demanding guest."[3]

In addition to the guilt I felt for not being able to muster the strength I had studied and witnessed, I had some convert baggage. We do bring along years of teaching on fear of death as well as our weeping and wailing grieving tendencies. Further, whatever DNA gives the British their stiff upper lip when it comes to the loss of loved ones apparently skipped me. Tears come when I hear Primary children sing—anything. Even when they shout "Book of Mormon Stories," I am in tears. With all their shuffling awkwardness, the deacons and teachers singing about the armies of Helaman still puts me over the top. I have a tender heart, a guilty conscience about grief, and a tendency to sob. That's a triple whammy.

As I searched the scriptures and talks for cures for my grief, I began to realize that what I was experiencing was not unique to converts. Despite the fact that we throw a great funeral, grief is real, even among our leaders. President Hinckley spoke in 1993 about his father's tenderness when his wife succumbed to cancer:

> That was sixty-two years ago, but I remember with clarity my brokenhearted father as he stepped off the train and greeted his grief-stricken children. We walked solemnly down the station platform to the baggage car, where the casket was unloaded and taken by the mortician. We came to know even more about the tenderness of our father's heart. This has had an effect on me all of my life.
>
> I also came to know something of death—the absolute devastation of children losing their mother—but also of peace without pain and the certainty that death cannot be the end of the soul.[4]

That second part of the quote became my focus—grief is real, but peace is possible. So, I undertook a study of grief and discovered that the best of the best have tried to tackle grief. The Joan Didion formula consists of weighing ninety pounds, writing for the *New Yorker*, and penning an entire book to ask, "Why me?" The ninety-pound body possibility was on a ship that sailed sometime during my junior-high-school years. I delivered late babies larger than that. And the *New Yorker* is unlikely to pick up the musings of a conservative Mormon. But I did understand her "Why me?" question. I was stuck there.

I found many books full of warnings about grief: "The first year is difficult." I already knew that, but I was on the second go-round of a first year. The standard book mantra was, "Grief is a process." The grief process consists of seven steps. Or is it twelve? Perhaps I have confused grief with addiction. Or have I? Perhaps we are somewhat addicted to the life we had before the loss of a loved one. And after about the seventh book—or was it the twelfth?—I had exhausted my patience with these grief writers and experts. Some wrote even without experiencing grief. This advice is akin to what you get from a marriage counselor who has never been married. Reality of the challenge may not be within their grasp.

The books and our Church teach us that we have those around us who will help: family, ward members, and friends. They were all there for the funeral, but no matter how terrific they are, they necessarily depart to trot down their daily paths of busyness. Because they have returned to their normal, they perhaps do not grasp that your life has been changed forever. You can't go back to that life even as they have returned to theirs. They become impatient with you and move surprisingly quickly into the "Get on with your life" lectures. To paraphrase Dr. Seuss, Oh! the suggestions you will hear! Oh! the activities they'll present, in the interest of getting you to "move on." "Plant a garden!" they will urge. There's a certain irony in this near-universal suggestion. In fact, I would proceed with the garden deal with caution, especially for those who have no horticultural experience. You just went through an experience of losing a living thing. Failed gardening means coping with sure and certain death of rutabagas. Also, as Neil Simon once commented, you can go to Europe for the cost of growing corn in your backyard. Why, I've killed growing carrots, something even that flirtyvixen Scarlett O'Hara could harvest in the midst of the Civil War, a burning Atlanta, and plundering Yankees.

When our Claire died, I knew I needed more than books, friends, counseling, and all the other poultices for sorrow. As people of profound faith, my husband and I know that our Claire has simply entered a new realm, a new phase of her eternal life. We also know that she is free of the physical shackles that so challenged and constrained her earthly existence. We, speaking in the language of two attorneys, know beyond a shadow of a doubt that we will see her again. As certainly as we know the sun rises, we know that she is well, progressing nicely in the perfection of her soul. This knowledge of her well-being is what loads of folks who have never lost a child offer as consolation and condolence, always with a dose of condescension.

The faith that offers the reassurance of life after death springs from the same tenderness, sensitivity, and depth that produce grief. A life that is dedicated to Christ demands empathy, a loving heart, and a caring soul. Those demands cannot be boxed away simply because of a profound testimony that there is eternal life. How could we have faith and not feel the loss of a loved one? C. S. Lewis wrote in *A Grief Observed*, "Who still thinks there is some device (if only he could find it) which will make pain not be pain?"[5] Clive Staples also said that you never really know what is truth or falsehood until it becomes a matter of life and death to you. The loss of a loved one is perhaps our final exam on our belief in eternal life.

I was taking that critical exam on my faith about the Resurrection and the plan of salvation, and many around me had not yet faced their test. A natural disconnect comes from this void in life—well, death—experience. Their expectations of me were, as a result, quite high. They want joy, laughter, and perhaps some reassurance from us that their as-yet-tested faith is well placed. There are still times when I wonder whether they could pass the exam. I have witnessed realignments of wards in a stake that resulted in weeping and wailing and more murmuring than was witnessed in Zion's Camp. Their faith was fine on the loss of my daughter but not so good when it came to losing a neighbor to another ward.

I could feel a wedge building in my faith. I heard someone say in a Sunday school class discussion recently, "If we really understood the gospel of Christ, there would never be any need for sadness." Spoken like a parent who has never lost a child. As Eliza R. Snow would say, the thought makes reason stare.[6] We cannot know joy unless we know its counterpart—sadness. Grief, Queen Elizabeth explained, is the price we pay for love. Even Job went through a tense period of wallowing: "Oh that my grief were thoroughly weighed, and my calamity laid in the balances together."[7] And, ultimately, we fall into the test that Heber C. Kimball has described, "Let me say to you, that many of you will see the time when you will have all the trouble, trial, and persecution you can stand...If you have not got the testimony, live right and call upon the Lord and cease not till you obtain it. If you do not, you will not stand. Remember these sayings...The time will come when no man nor woman will be able to endure on borrowed light. If you do not have it, how can you stand?"[8] I had a little work to do in order to stand on my own, but I had to do it with the delicate balance of missing both my mother and daughter. I read on the Cigna website on grief, one of hundreds I would turn to following Claire's death, that you cannot avoid "the bill of pain." Grief is painful and we have to go through it in order to get to healing. I didn't want to avoid the pain; I was confused as to whether I was allowed to experience it.

I knew the sense of loss and sorrow were also part of our divine heritage. How could we profess to deserve His love if we did not feel the loss of a precious one? We know from the allegory of Enos that the Lord of the vineyard feels acutely the spiritual loss of his loved ones, "It grieveth me that I should lose this tree,"[9] and "...the Lord of the vineyard wept, and said unto the servant, 'What more could I have done for my vineyard?'"[10] How could we carry the tenderness that His admonitions require of us unless we felt grief acutely? How could we not weep at the loss of a loved one?

So grief is possible, it's real, and it happens to the most faithful. Neither the trite offerings of those who had not felt our pain nor the strength of our conviction to Christ and His gift of eternal life provided the solace I needed for getting through this process glibly referred to as "grieving." When I turned to those of faith for help, they offered the doctrine I truly did already understand. When I turned to those not of faith, they offered doses of secular solutions, "Try to get some exercise and eat right," "Reach out to others," or, my personal favorite, "Find yourself again in a new hobby." If you turn to professionals, grief counselors, then you will get a lot of expensive listening. All in all these groups meant well, but they all just made me want to say, "You're not helping."

This journey from the abnormality of the loss of a child following so quickly on the heels of the loss of my mother was a challenge for my faith. Losing a child runs contra to natural order. The enormity of my task seemed to escape so many around me. I felt like Jack Nicholson's character in *As Good As It Gets*, Melvin Udall, who sought help from a friend for his agony over his unrequited love for "Carol the Waitress." His well-intentioned friend resorted to platitudes. Unaided and only abetted in his emotional state of confusion and angst, Melvin chastised his friend, "Look, you, I'm very intelligent. If you're going to give me advice or conversation or consolation or hope, you got to be better than you're doing." Melvin added, "I'm drowning here, and you're describing the water!"

I heard a great deal about H_2O during the months after Claire left us. I needed a lifeline, and folks were yelling to me from the shore, "You either have to swim or you'll sink!" The principles of physics and I were one. But, for a time, I just needed to tread water, the metaphor that describes perfectly where you are: in the tricky waters and undertow of grief. We know from Doctrine and Covenants 61 that Satan is there on the waters, in control, and we are vulnerable. It occurred to me that he was using the injustice of the loss of a child. He picked up on a weakness and perceived my Achilles' heel, and he was seizing the moment.

We are quite strong in keeping the commandments and resisting the temptations about which we are warned, nearly every conference. Fidelity in marriage, attending our meetings, keeping the Sabbath day holy—these are the kinds of things that are clear in their direction and, with discipline, well executed. Satan often doesn't stand a chance in weakening us with these straightforward areas. But Elder Oaks has warned us, "Like the fabled Achilles, who was immune to every lethal blow except to his heel, many of us have a special weakness that can be exploited to our spiritual downfall."[11] I had the odd spiritual weakness, one of refusal to accept a loss despite the promise of eternal life. How odd that too much tenderness and my struggle with grief could chip away at my testimony! President Romney reminds us, "Satan's methods are various, devious, and countless."[12]

But I did find my way back to shore. I went to the cemetery every day for the first year after our Claire died, give or take an additional 180 days. I had a journey of conquering grief—my 365 steps, or maybe 545, which were my recovery program among the headstones. Given that AA has cured many a soul of addiction with twelve steps, my program is not ideal and needed a little refinement. Out of respect for your time and publisher budgets, I narrowed the recovery program to one thought for each of the fifty-two weeks. These were the thoughts, the insights, the revelations, and the assurances that came to me in the cemetery or because of my visits there. From the stories of how I happened to discover the cemetery as a form of extreme grief therapy to what happened while I was visiting are here.

But the stories are not focused on the loss. The story here is the healing and the newfound strength in my testimony. I found the power of healing, but I also found the plan of salvation was real, not just a rote thought to be repeated because we hear others say so and we lean on them. The stories of my cemetery visits are as varied as the lives of those who share the graveyard turf with our Claire. But they are all stories that came my way because I visited my daughter's grave each day. Each story proved to be a building block for a stronger faith. Each story also brought gratitude for the blessings that were being sent from a loving Heavenly Father to save me from

Satan's flaxen cord that had found its way around my neck through the seemingly innocent feelings of sadness.[13]

So, I offer you my unique fifty-two-step antigrief program, developed among the headstones. I'm no Ezekiel, but the Havisham dress is off, the house is presentable, and I even have a garden. The carrots were harvested at a pencil-like width, but the rutabagas were to die for.

1

THE FUNERAL AND
THE CEMETERY AMBLE

We laid our daughter Claire to rest on January 17, 2007. The day was a cold one for Arizona, but sunny, different from the usual January rain and gloom that had been with us when we picked out and purchased her burial plot. My husband, Terry, gave the dedicatory prayer at the graveside, and that was it—the casket was going into the ground. When cemetery workers lower a vault, there seems to be creaking, real or imagined. The physical presence of our daughter, who left this life just ten days shy of her twentieth birthday, was gone, buried in a well-chosen white casket and silver vault. Those latter choices proved elegant and inspired, despite our novice nature with the funeral business.

Oddly, what I can remember from that day and what caught my attention were the graveside activities. At the grave, people behave as novice actors and actresses on the stage—they don't quite know where to stand or what to do with their hands, and they have clearly forgotten their lines, if they ever knew them. People mull about as they wait for the graveside prayer. As folks walked from their parked cars, I noticed a certain amble. It occurred to me that day that people never walk briskly in a cemetery. There is a demand for respect on this occasion that makes even the most scheduled and electronically connected folks stroll. Something about a cemetery reminds us to slow down and inspires the appropriate awe: your days are numbered.

I had my first cemetery insight before I knew how much of a role it would play in helping me to make sense of our loss. No matter who loses whom and regardless of whether the timing is right, wrong, or just plain unjust, you revisit your own life. The loss of a loved one starts a fascinating introspection, an introspection that gives you the ultimate freedom of not caring. When some friends of our lost their toddler son, they found themselves sitting out on the front lawn with their insulated Maverick store cups for hours at a time. The rest of the world was passing them by on a moving sidewalk, and they did not yet want to rejoin them. They wanted to cherish the time of being free from the world's demands. It's not that you don't care about anything. It is a "not caring" about the wrong things or a caring about the right things—however you want to phrase it. Grief is a process all right—a process of learning.

Preloss and prefuneral, you were worried about whether to buy a new car. Postloss you want to keep the old car for so many reasons: your loved one rode in that car; that car took you to some mighty important events; that car is broken in—you can eat anything in that car and not worry; you can't take the new car with you; and, most important, in the next life we will not be able to distinguish ourselves by the model, make, or year of the car we drive. I imagine that in the next life there are probably only Yugos—a car that just screams, "Really don't care much about what gets me there; I just need transportation." Actually, the car screams more loudly, "This is what you get when the government builds cars," but that's a book for another time.

The ambling I saw among friends and relatives in the cemetery the day of the funeral started me down a path of self-reform on priorities. That journey has been remarkable because after years of post-Claire introspection, I have life narrowed down to two types of problems: fixable and nonfixable. Psychiatrists and counselors earn the big bucks, or at least regularity of small bucks, because people have too many classifications for their problems. They are also on a pointless quest of trying to fix the nonfixable and fretting over and delaying the fixes for the fixable.

You need an example. If a water pipe bursts in your home and floods it, as a neighbor's did during my year of the cemetery, you have a huge problem. You have an expensive problem. You have a problem that may find you living with your four children in one room or in an Econo Lodge for a few nights. You have a problem that will take some time to fix. You have a problem that will find you dealing with insurance agents and contractors, in all their glory. You have a problem that produces stress, raises blood pressure, and, even in the most faithful, will find a few swears escaping here and there. But, you have a fixable problem. The neighbor said she understood how I felt about our loss of Claire after her water pipe burst because it was so hard. Nope—just a bit of confusion there. Not only can the pipe and the house be fixed, but there is the added bonus of a new floor. Just think! Wood floors and new carpet! Plus, you have a great story about the whole process, from water circulating around your feet as you walked down the hallway from your bedroom one morning to the contractor you had to go pick up to come to work each day because the bank repossessed his truck. Colorful problem. Challenging problem. Pain-in-the-neck problem. Big problem, but big *fixable* problem.

Without the funeral amble to remind us, we tend to list all the "woe-is-me" events in our lives and feel put-upon. We are stressed, challenged, and possessed of a Job complex because we can't break the issues down into their simplistic bicameral structure: fixable and nonfixable.

When the problem is fixable, continue your amble. Just roll up your sleeves and get at it. Work and endure, with good cheer. When the problem is nonfixable, amble and do your introspection. I had a nonfixable problem when our Claire left us. I could get all the new flooring, even rising to the level of Travertine, and Claire would still be gone. But I was given the blessing of a forced and continuing amble. My job was to retain the cemetery gait and figure out the take-aways, as they say in corporate meetings and training, from a profound loss. In the fixable problems, we gain experience and learn the skill of good cheer in challenging times. Oh, but the nonfixables are where we gain our depth. There is no contractor to call, no replacement to be found, and we must search instead for understanding. A fixable problem is a challenge that is fixed and how soon we forget the help we had in persevering. So fleeting is the challenge and, with time, so easy its resolution seems in hindsight. Sometimes we gain confidence from the fixing. Too often we take on arrogance because the fixable is fixed and we move along.

One of the things I have learned in my research at the university over the years is that the businesspeople most likely to get into trouble are those who are known as "Mr. or Ms. Fix-It." These are the businesspeople who have made careers and much money from stepping into situations and always finding a way to fix the problem. Despite their skill, however, they are missing the experience of hitting a wall—one of those situations in which the remedy is not as easy or may just be elusive. Finding it difficult to step down from their pedestal of recognition and achievement, they will cross legal and ethical lines to get a quick fix. They had not developed the patience to work at a problem for the long term and they did not have the humility to admit that they needed help on a new and different problem. They have the classic Greek tragedy problem of hubris. My Heavenly Father was giving me the blessing of hitting a wall. A wall that required time to study. A wall that required something other than my breakneck pace. A wall that I was not going to get over without His help. Ironic that as an academic I could see the mote in business executive's eyes when it came to their handling of wall problems, but I missed the beam in my own eye when it came to my own.[14]

A nonfixable problem stays with us and challenges us to find a way through its heavy weight. It does take some serious ambling to understand the nonfixable, and ambling with heavy weight is slower. A miracle healing is a beautiful thing and a faith builder for many. But the search for the answer as to why you were not given the miracle healing is a much slower faith builder.

President George Q. Cannon described the irony of those who rely on the instant miracles: "It has been a matter of remark among those who have had experience in this Church that where men have been brought into the Church by such manifestations, it has required a constant succession of them to keep them in the Church; their faith has had to be constantly strengthened by witnessing some such manifestations; but where they have been convinced by the outpouring of the spirit of God,...they have been more likely to stand, more likely to endure persecution and trial than those who have been convinced through some supernatural manifestation."[15] If you study Church history you find that so many of the brethren who had those instantaneous conversions, complete with visions, even being witnesses to angels, would later struggle in the Church. They had not had the Crock-Pot, slow-cooker conversion that comes from tests and trials.

I had prayed for my daughter to live. I received my answer, and the answer was no. However, I had been given the gift of no miracle cure for my daughter. I was being asked to seek an outpouring of the Spirit through this process of grief. Those who refer to grief as a process may be correct; what they are missing is what's being processed. Sometimes it takes 365 days or so just to understand the question. And the question is: what am I supposed to be learning from this? I had my first lesson, just from the cemetery amble.

2

ROSENCRANTZ AND GUILDENSTERN

The first time you set foot in a cemetery, you will see them. They are there, daily, except Sundays, the gravediggers. Save it be when we read or watch *Hamlet,* we don't think much about those who must carve out the requisite six-foot-deep burial plots. Hamlet is offended when he witnesses the gravediggers singing as they go about preparing what will be Ophelia's grave. The Bard and Hamlet had a morbid view of gravediggers. They are really quite helpful people when it comes to grief. Shakespeare didn't know gravediggers as I know gravediggers.

There are three schools of thought on gravediggers. One group does not think about them. To subscribe to this behavioral theory, you think not of their shovels and digging. You really do not want to know who works at a cemetery and how the graves get dug. So you imagine that elves or extraterrestrials have been given the assignment to produce prepared burial plots. No human, in your mind, would be involved in such skullduggery, or, more aptly, skulldiggery.

The second school of thought just ignores the gravediggers. Unlike the first, they do not fancy UFOs depositing charming chaps for the evening so that they can dig away, heigh-ho, heigh-ho. They acknowledge the existence of earthly, as it were, gravediggers, but because of their grief they have developed disdain for fellows who facilitate a "final resting" place. They want nothing more to do with the fellows. They make no eye contact and speak not to these employees at the cemetery. I believe this noncommunicative group reasons that if you speak with a gravedigger, they will get the wrong idea and conclude that you are greasing the skids with them because you too will soon be in need of their services. There's a certain sincere logic here with their belief that if you shun those who work at the cemetery you won't have to take death's call. It's a line of self-preservation reasoning that goes like this, "I don't really know anyone at the cemetery, so why would I want to live there?" Start chatting it up with the gravediggers, you suddenly have friends in strange places, and you have become too comfortable in a place you don't like and don't want to be, yet.

The third school of thought is the one to which I gravitated, from the day of the funeral. My first epiphany on gravediggers occurred at Claire's interment. When it came time to lower her casket and vault into the ground, Rosencrantz and Guildenstern appeared, clad in their navy work pants and light blue shirts. However, they had taken the time to put on a tie. In this day and age, when parents attend college graduations in jogging suits, these city workers cared enough to button their top shirt button and put on a tie. They were not clip-on ties either—these ties were the real thing. I was so deeply touched by this courtesy, this showing of respect for her and for us, Claire's family. Only sensitivity born of experience could have ingrained in them this gracious tradition.

Shortly after Claire's funeral, I wrote a note to the cemetery director as well as the city manager to thank them for the cemetery workers' professionalism and sensitivity. I mentioned the ties. When we are stumbling through a loss, just knowing that others care touches our tender hearts. They cared enough to put on a tie. They would spend the day digging, moving earth, lugging vaults, fixing sprinklers, and emptying trash. But for my daughter, they spruced up, tie and all. Respect, sensitivity, kindness—how dare Shakespeare call them clowns in his *Hamlet*!

A soothing salve for grief is gratitude. When I researched gratitude as a topic of our Church leaders, I found an interesting connection between gratitude and gait—back to the amble. President Gordon B. Hinckley said, "When you walk with gratitude, you do not walk with arrogance and conceit and egotism, you walk with a spirit of thanksgiving that is becoming to you and will bless your lives."[16] You amble. You take the time to notice the ties on gravediggers. They cared enough to look their best for us.

My cemetery was offering me the richness of the human condition. Grief is difficult, but it shouldn't blind us to the gestures of those who offer their respect and kindness. On the day of Claire's funeral, I did not realize how many more times Rosencrantz and Guildenstern would bless my life and help with my healing.

3

THE FIRST TRIP BACK TO THE CEMETERY

After the bizarre postfuneral meal (who can eat?) and the exit of friends and family, the loneliness of being parents who have lost a child sets in. Siblings are resilient. With a day free from school, they turned to their friends. Terry and I rattled about a house that was missing one of its longstanding occupants. As dusk crept upon us, the same concerns and resulting impulse hit us simultaneously. What if they didn't put the dirt on the grave right? What if they forgot the flowers? What if no one followed through on finishing the tasks that Hamlet-like grave fellows do? Knowing that the gates closed when darkness falls, we drove immediately to the cemetery.

Although we had picked out Claire's plot, chosen an additional two plots for us right next to it, and held a graveside service there, we still found ourselves lost as we searched for our daughter's grave. The bizarre rollable awning that had covered us during the graveside service was no longer there. That rolling behemoth was our North Star, and Rosencrantz and Guildenstern had moved it. The simple white chairs that had held us when weak knees gave out had been returned to storage. Fresh flowers, we thought. Hone in on fresh flowers. Success! There was Claire's grave, alone in the midst of a new section of the cemetery, covered with sprays and wreaths.

Terry had brought along his camera. The man is never without a camera for an awkward moment. When I have not yet spackled on makeup to my increasingly moonlike facial surface, when I am bending over without bent knees, he is there, camera at the ready. You have just received a small glimpse of his diabolical nature. So, of course, he brought his camera to the cemetery. Yet I did not chastise him this time for an inopportune Kodak moment because, for some reason, I wanted to remember what the flowers from Claire's funeral looked like.

There's another thing few folks discuss with you as you grieve. You really will want to remember things from the funeral. You can't recall the visuals—how things looked. You waddle through these events in shock. But there comes a point when you want to remember. Shock does funny things to you, but when the shock goes away, you want to see what you missed. Terry took a picture of me by the grave with all those flowers, something I glance at today and am grateful to have. Looking at those flowers—the baskets and standing sprays, I have a record of how many cared for and about us during a time that would otherwise remain a blur. You can't process that love and caring during acute pain, but you can look back and see the blessing of friends who cared enough to send the very best. And a poultice for grief is the knowledge that there are those who do love and care for you even when their awkwardness about death prevents them from talking with you about your loss.

As darkness fell and we stood next to the dirt that covered our daughter's earthly remains, Terry and I both felt better. This strange and impetuous act of coming back to the cemetery on the day of our youngest daughter's funeral had brought, oddly, some comfort. We were, once again, still just parents, checking on a child who was spending the night elsewhere. Actually, she was spending the night in two different places, but we were only qualified to check on her in just one. One location was a place beyond this earth, one that we were not yet permitted to enter. Her other locale, this cemetery, her resting place, was something we could see. Better yet, we were just checking on her before lights out. Granted, a child's bedroom does have a slightly different feel to it from a cemetery. But, we were, for those brief moments in the cemetery that first evening, parents once again to our departed daughter.

That night, and many times since, I have studied Section 137 of the Doctrine and Covenants and its promise to parents who lose a child before the age of accountability. I learned that our parenting days for Claire were not nearly done. Our Claire was nearly twenty, but because of her disabilities, she had the mental development of a three-to-six-month-old. Verse 10 reads, "And I also beheld that all children who die before they arrive at the years of accountability are saved in the celestial kingdom of heaven." Bruce R. McConkie provides further explanation and assurance to parents with a quote from Joseph F. Smith, "'You will have the joy, the pleasure, and satisfaction of nurturing this child, after its resurrection, until it reaches the full stature of its spirit.' There is restitution, there is growth, there is development, after the resurrection from death. I love this truth. It speaks volumes of happiness, of joy and gratitude to my soul. Thank the Lord he has revealed these principles to us."[17]

4

HOOKED ON AND HELPED BY THE CEMETERY

Following that first-night visit to the cemetery, sleeplessness found me wading through the grief books and their vapid consolations. Tired of their shallowness, I found the best advice in an odd source. I began rereading portions of David McCullough's book *John Adams*. You can strike a history buff with grief, but you will never take the buff out of her history. I ran across the advice I needed on grief from Thomas Jefferson. Jefferson writes a mean Declaration of Independence, but the man also understood grief. When John Adams lost his beloved Abigail, after over half a century of marriage, Adams renewed his friendship with Jefferson through a letter that exposed his broken heart and how difficult it was to grapple with the "heavy afflictions" of the loss of Abigail. Jefferson wrote back, "Time and silence are the only medicines."[18]

Jeffersonian democracy and attitudes on federalism and my views have not always been one, but he is right about loss, grief, and recovery. Possessed of the moral authority of having lost a child and his wife in one year, Mr. Jefferson's concise advice was just the ticket.

Jefferson never said exactly how much time was necessary. My experience tells me that time is the variable in the Jefferson formula. But the silence concept was a fairly clear one. Yet, silence is not achieved easily for ours is not a world of quiet. We are iPodded, cell-phoned, and Blackberried to such an extent that we ignore those who are right there with us, in person. Mr. Jefferson was reminding his friend of the need for detachment from bustle. We also find ourselves cursed with, crossing into, and engaged in conversations that are not even ours. Why do we worry about the federal government eavesdropping under the Patriot Act? I hear too-much-information conversations each day. Conversations about affairs, dates, boils, too-big-thighs (from men and women and you figure out who's saying what) and just generally too much Old Testament debauchery. I hear these conversations all day, every day—too much mindless yammering and too little quiet.

To find Jeffersonian silence, you must find a spot where there are folks who come sans electronic devices. The only place on earth where its occupants are not WiFied or possessed of customized ringers, earbuds, headphones, or "you've got mail" advisories is the cemetery. Its occupants may well be communicating, but they are not using cell phone towers. And if they are listening to music, only dogs can hear it, and canines are banished from cemeteries, so no chance of them singing along. Silence, blessed Jeffersonian silence, could be mine at the graveyard.

I had already had several remarkable insights at the cemetery, so why not? Truth be told, I went every day for eighteen months. When I finished writing this book, I only then reached a point where I didn't go each day. But, I have evolved. In the beginning I went to the cemetery trying to escape reality. I wanted somehow to feel, as a mother, that I was doing something to help my daughter, even if it was simply checking on her grave. By the end, I had trouble not going because this cemetery had been the place where I was healed. Our place, Claire and I. Together we made the journey of transition, from a life we had together to our divinely imposed separation and two different lives. Children do leave home all the time, but you hear from them once in a while with an update, generally accompanied by a request for funds. You have an inkling of how things are going, and you can always pick up the phone and call and have others listen in as you chat with them at some inopportune moment. I have overheard a few of those conversations as well, the ones in which parents begin, "You never call, you never visit, you never write…"

But the tender feelings I experienced at the cemetery made it difficult to not go because it felt so comfortable. Even if I just did a drive-by, there was a certain peace, a reassurance I had found there. Folks weren't kidding when they came up with that "rest in peace" phrase. I just didn't know that peace came to the survivors. In that quiet solitude, I found answers and strength.

There were times during the first year following Claire's death when relatives and friends would express concern about my daily treks. "You're gettin' weird here, Marianne." I had a certain respect for these kindly worriers. They, by their own admission, had no solution, but they had the fortitude to speak their minds. There were, however, many sages such as those who, upon hearing of the daily cemetery visits, would offer, "Perhaps some medication would help." Poor misguided souls. Then I'd be dealing with my grief and the added problem of addiction. Nay, masking the pain was simply postponing the pain. I was facing it all—head-on—each day at the cemetery.

Being children of the sixties, Terry and I had a great many friends with the Woody Allen obsession that therapy was as necessary to life as a good breakfast. When informed of my cemetery ritual, the Woody Allen friends offered me the same ubiquitous presence that they had in their own lives: "You really need some counseling." I avoided counseling for a very logical reason. I knew what the counselor would say. "Get used to it. That's $148 for today." I knew the task I had been assigned—get used to it—I just had to find a way, my way. If nothing else, at least until early 2008, gas to the cemetery was cheaper than therapy.

So, the cemetery, unconventional though it may have been, became my coping mechanism, my counseling, my psychotropic medication, and all-in-one-form of extreme therapy. The cemetery saw me through that awful first year, with no counseling, no drugs, and no alcohol. Perhaps there were one or two too many Diet Cokes along the journey, but I emerged from that first year having functioned well. Not one day was spent in bed. Not one day found me unshowered—I always had the cemetery to visit. Respect for Claire would not allow me to go there unless I looked my best.

Through this remarkable journey of a year-plus, I emerged with insight and strength. The loss of a child is a challenge unlike any other loss. You would lay down your life for your child, but you could not save her. No matter how valiant the effort, parents who lose a child still cope with the questions of, "What if?" and the resulting feeling of parental failure. It's a parent's job to protect, help, nurture, and all with no time deadlines. But death took away that role. Justice is violated. Mercy is absent.

The cemetery was different—communication there required a spiritual connection. Seeking the spirit is one and the same as seeking knowledge, affirmation, and comfort. There is a reason that "Ponder" comes in between "Search" and "Pray." Elder Gene R. Cook did a careful analysis of Moroni 10:3 and the last five words, which include the word "ponder."[19] And his insight was what I found in the cemetery: "[Moroni] is talking about the step of *receiving the teachings* contained in that which we have read—considering them or *receiving* them into our minds and hearts so that we can ponder them in order to be prepared for the next step, which is to accept an answer from our Heavenly Father."[20] There are no answers without the pondering. We tend to forget the pondering if it isn't placed smack-dab in the middle of the song or Moroni's advice. It took me a year to figure out what that short sentence just described, but it was Jeffersonian time well spent. Mine were really not cemetery visits; they were cemetery ponderings.

5

ROSENCRANTZ AND GUILDENSTERN—REDUX

Never miss a chance to talk with a gravedigger. Few people (who are alive) have as much experience with death as gravediggers. Even fewer people alive have their wisdom.

Just think of the magnificent gossip to which they have access. Each day they learn who has died. They are there for every funeral. They witness human emotion at its rawest. They see the feuding relatives come together or stand apart at the graveside services. They know who sent flowers. They could tell you how many people showed up for each funeral. They can tell you who got to ride in the limo. They can see who lingers behind when others have had enough. And they know who comes to which graves and how often.

My dear gravediggers, my Rosencrantz and Guildenstern humorists, should be writing this book. Their jobs have given them insight, perspective, and an ability to counsel the grieving that would embarrass most psychiatrists. Few learned docs have been able to help as many troubled souls as my gravediggers. Furthermore, they do it daily despite no provision in their job descriptions for "therapeutic counseling of the bereaved." They just offer it as an additional service.

They waved to me each day. When they were near Claire's grave, they stopped to talk. They always asked how I was doing. As time went by, they even felt comfortable enough to ask me about Claire's life and death. They became my caring friends who had a built-in sense of the perfect thing to say to someone who is visiting the grave of her daughter.

I also understood from their presence that we are blessed by the angels among us, people who are sent our way to help. They are on an errand of mercy. Rosencrantz and Guildenstern were so kind to me that I often found myself staring at their clothing and going home and wondering aloud to my husband one day whether they might be two of the Three Nephites.[21]

My gravediggers were simply part of the angels among us. Joseph Fielding Smith wrote, "the eyes of God and his angels and of every man who dwells in the celestial world are watching us and the courses we pursue."[22] Indeed, they are, and, often, they send help in the most extraordinary disguises.

6

ANNA: A WIDOW'S TALE

That first evening when we returned to the cemetery, as we were standing by Claire's grave, along came a widow who had been visiting her husband's grave. She had lost her husband on January 1, 2007, and since we were at January 11 for our loss and now January 17 for the funeral, she was an old-timer in cemetery experience. She really did seem so wise. Then again, anyone who had been to a funeral home other than for a wake was more experienced than we. Tiny and thin, with a presence that reeked of efficiency and all-organic foods, this widow, Anna, would soon become our first cemetery friend. I had somehow imagined cemeteries as silent places where folks only nodded at each other, just as sullen and mute undertakers act toward everyone. Being the inexperienced ones in the funeral and burial processes, I assumed that we were to take our cues from the veterans. Sullen and mute was the etiquette message I got from the undertakers. They even roped us off from the other families who happened to be going through their loss. Communication about the bereaved appeared to be verboten.

But undertakers are dealing with their jobs, not grief. I imagine that out of habit undertakers become like the grocery store checkout clerk—very polite as they roll through the same motions each day with a stream of customers rattling through. Grieving relatives probably all look the same to undertakers after a while. But personal and individual grief demands something more than that restrained behavior of the undertaker with all his muted tones. They take muted all the way to black, which is what all undertakers wear. Oddly, they have white hearses now. I wonder who came up with the black-and-white combo. I also wondered if, in their wild moments, undertakers don navy pinstripe suits for painting the town.

Anna helped me realize that I misunderstood cemetery, grief, and funeral protocol if I was taking my cues from undertakers. I indeed did have many postfuneral protocol questions for which there is no book. And just try Googling "postfuneral protocol" and note that you have stumped Sergey and Brin or Page and Engine or whoever those Google guys are. What exactly is proper protocol at a cemetery when you are there for a purpose other than the funeral itself? Anna had the answers. She came bouncing over to Terry and me on our first visit, offering to take a picture of the both of us by Claire's flowers because, she assured us with all the experience of ten extra days of mourning, "You will want to have a record of this day and this moment."

Here was the voice of experience. Finally, six days after Claire's death and six hours after her funeral, we had advice from someone who understood. Undertakers keep you separated from other customers (if that's what you call those of us buying caskets and vaults and programs). I am not sure why, but undertakers behave as if you need to be quarantined from others who have lost loved ones. We are not allowed to see the people who are in the other rooms at the funeral parlor. Yet, I wanted to have a conversation with them along the lines of those we had in high school with the first-period students after a hard algebra test, to wit, "Do you have to know quadratic equations?" "How hard was it?" I wanted to ask the others who were struggling with the funeral experience, "Did you get the vault or the concrete pad and shell?"

But now, in the cemetery, we had no undertaker rope lines or supervision and all bets were off. We could compare notes, share stories, and ease each others' pain. Anna told us the story of her husband's passing, her deep love for him, and that she had come to the cemetery every day since his funeral because it made her feel better. What we had in common was that her husband, just like our Claire, was taken too soon. She also understood the difficult memories of being there at the time of passing, of witnessing the last breaths of a loved one.

22

Through that first visit and Anna's concern, I got more lessons of the cemetery—first, the people there are willing to speak of the unspeakable. As C. S. Lewis noted, "Why has no one told me these things?"[23] Second, the people there really do need to speak the unspeakable. Like me, folks at the cemetery want more than the trite thoughts of the inexperienced.

Anna had so much tangible advice to offer. We walked over to see her husband's grave. There was a little tin grave marker that had his name, date of birth, and date of death. She explained that his real stone marker (something I always called a "tombstone" or a "headstone") would take time and "for forty dollars, this little sign is worth it so his grave is marked until the stone arrives." No more trouble finding Claire's grave even after the flowers were gone because we could get the tiny, temporary tin plate courtesy of Anna's advice.

The cemetery is like a concert, something people go to for different reasons. Some people are there for the social interaction and some people want to see the artist perform live. Seeing all the folks alive at the cemetery is a tall order, but there is a surprising amount of social interaction. The cemetery is also like church—some people are there for the social interaction and some people want answers about what happens beyond this life. Those seeking answers find that the cemetery just has an admission requirement: you must feel a tender connection with someone residing there, and it must be enough of a connection that you return to visit, a visit that can only be symbolic until the next life.

Folks at the cemetery share a common bond. They lost someone and they feel the pain. It is irrelevant whether it is the day of the funeral or Memorial Day five years later; they are still there because they lost someone they loved and it hurts. Sometimes they come to cry. Sometimes they come to ponder. But they are all there because of the common bond of a loss. Because of this shared and uniform purpose, the cemetery is a library for those in mourning. Everyone there is a librarian who can provide or direct you to some helpful information. Standing there that first night with Anna and Terry, I could not have imagined how many more cemetery librarians I would meet, how many more lessons the cemetery would offer, and how much information I could be directed to that would help me.

I still see Anna, sometimes at the cemetery, and sometimes in the temple, where she is a worker. We are both busy, active, and faithful. When I see her I smile because I know something that no one else around knows—that she was there with her wisdom and kindness when a struggling mother needed help. Elder Merrill Bateman wrote about the presence of angels whenever there has been a new dispensation of the gospel, at the time of the Savior's birth and as the Prophet Joseph Smith was being instructed. But, Elder Bateman also noted that there comes a time when the Lord turns over the work of angels to those on the earth: "...as time elapses and the number of faithful members increases, more is expected of those in mortality. For example, when a new country is opened to the gospel, missionaries learn that many have been prepared in miraculous ways to receive the gospel, and miracles occur with some frequency to advance the work. Once a core of members is established, however, the Lord's assistance changes as He provides opportunities for the members to become the miracle workers."[24] I had miracle workers sent my way. Sometimes we miss the angels sent to us to help because we are so busy. I was never too busy at the cemetery and the angels made their moves there.

7

NIGHT OF THE LIVING DEAD

At this point, there are more than a few of you who may be thinking that a cemetery is just, well, creepy. Who would want to frequent such a spot? Before Claire died, I had only two forms of exposure to graveyards. The first derived from that weird B-grade (more like D-grade) movie classic: *Night of the Living Dead*. The *NOTLD* graveyard involves unexplained wind gusts engulfing you even as creatures hide behind giant poplar trees, ready to pounce and take you wherever it is that ghouls haul off the innocent relatives of the departed who have the temerity to show up at their ghoulish stomping grounds. However, my more horrific perception of cemeteries came from Michael Jackson's "Thriller" video, complete with mummies unwinding from their tape or binding or whatever it is that wraps them up. There the mummies and greatly chopped-up ghouls were boogying alongside "The Gloved One" wearing their ragged designer clothing and displaying Gene Kelly's grace. Considering they were missing great chunks of their skulls as well as their muscle layers and a good part of their skin, they were fine disco dancers. Who would have guessed that when we were watching the "Thriller" video in the 1980s that the way the dancers looked in it were simply foreshadowings of what poor Michael Jackson, with all of his problems, would look like in the year 2000?

The graveyards in *NOTLD* and "Thriller" both look as if they were cobbled together when Salem had to do something with the remains of witches because the church graveyards wouldn't take them, to wit, "No witches here. Don't even think about it, Hester!" In the Salem cemeteries, the headstones are tilted and crooked. Names on them are partially eroded. *NOTLD* and "Thriller" cemeteries are also strategically located at enough distance from civilization that no living person sees or reports the great number of ghouls perched by cemetery trees or hears the screams of the captured grieving relatives. "Creepy" is the same adjective I once used almost exclusively for describing graveyards.

As it turns out, MTV and independent film producers of the B–D-grade film genre have greatly exaggerated death's sting. The graveyard of today has been stripped of superstition. The haunted house feel is gone. There must be a master's degree in graveyard management that has incorporated psychology, Zen, and a little bit of Ritz-Carlton service attitude. Think "park" with no Frisbees, no dogs, no couples who need to get a room, and, no ghouls. Part of the master's degree study must be a course on banishing counts, vampires, and other ill-clad ghosts. One last thing about the master's degree cemetery: think quiet. Oh, the wind does come, but these are breezes of peace that dry tears and push back tresses from foreheads hung in sadness. The breezes are reassuring blessings sent to provide movement and offer the sense that life does exist beyond the burial grounds. I have come to believe that graveyard breezes are strategic, sent from above when those seeking comfort need something to buoy their faith in life beyond this earth.

There is hardly a better remedy than standing near the grave of a loved one if you want to follow Jefferson's advice on silence. Your mind races, initially, about the void. In the first few months, body sobs would set in as I stared at the headstone with my daughter's name on it. That remained an out-of-body experience for months. Seeing your child's name on a headstone is like being Ebenezer Scrooge. The only thing missing as you look at that surreal, etched-in-stone name is an apparition pointing a finger for you to look and "Mark it well." You find yourself wishing that you could have Scrooge's second chance.

But with enough visits and time in that silence near her headstone, I found I couldn't stop the smiles. My mind would not allow me to recall the last few minutes of Claire's life. Those too-real memories of last breaths vanished as what made Claire and me laugh took over. I stepped into a different world when I entered the cemetery, maybe a world closer to her. She is there. Not as a ghoul because she always had exquisite taste in clothes. In the peace of that garden-like cemetery I could feel her and, eventually, all that was good about our time together returned with a vivacity that supplanted the trauma that was part of her last few weeks. I got to the point where I didn't even think about intubation, intensive care, and undertakers. Claire lives on, and I became acutely aware of that because of these quiet moments of recalling her vibrant life in my post-*NOTLD* cemeteries.

We miss the beauty around us when we are focused on what's wrong with our lives and the world. It's a glass half-full/half-empty framing of the issue. As we think in our hearts, so we are.[25] "Negative thinking patterns cause negative emotions; they can even trigger depression."[26] When we have a negative style of thinking, we have trouble seeing the good. Once I saw the beauty in the cemetery, I had some answers as well as an antidote to the sadness. Beginning with "creepy" was perhaps a tad on the negative side. When I realized how much care and effort went into these quiet places of contemplation, a simple question came to mind: Why would we devote this much time and effort to cemeteries if we were not expecting great things from the attention and care? The dividends included providing a quiet spot for loved ones and exquisite locations for the morning of the first Resurrection—when Claire would be with us again. For an event that is that important, you do need a place of peace, purity, and beauty.

8

THE PEOPLE WE LOOK RIGHT THROUGH...AND WHAT WE MISS

Later, as I got to know them, my gravediggers explained to me two very strong emotions that they felt. They feel they can make a difference in the lives of those who are trying to cope with life's greatest challenge: the loss of a loved one. But the other emotion my dear Rosencrantz expressed so ruefully, "People seem to look right through us, ignore us, and we are really trying to make it better and easier for them."

My gravediggers taught me that in our busy-ness or maybe because of perceived class distinctions or maybe because we just take things for granted, we do look right through people. What we take for granted is someone else's pride and joy. I realized that just the simple distraction of writing that first note of thanks to the gravediggers for their ties pushed me along the road to recovery. An outward focus of gratitude for the little acts of dignity and professionalism of others gets rid of the "me, me, me." Like opera singers doing daily warm-ups, we are addicted to the "mi, mi mi." How many times I have said to someone, "I was going to write a note and thank you, but..." But what? "But I got busy," "But I had to..." Now I wish I could go back and recapture those missed opportunities to thank the people I have looked right through.

During the time you are writing a thank-you note, you have to be focused on someone other than yourself. You can't wallow in your own problem when you are thinking of words of praise for others. In our fast-lane lives, we forget the value of a simple thank-you. When my gravediggers shared with me their tender feelings about how they are often ignored, I made a commitment—to be certain to find some way to recognize someone each day for the thankless and/or unnoticed jobs that they do. In a world of bristling souls, use the magic of a thank-you to change lives. I know this simple step changed mine. This outward focus found me busily and happily occupied in thanks and gratitude. When someone holds a door open, "That's kind of you," changes countenances. An offer to help a young mother struggling to fold her stroller on the Jetway as she holds her baby will find you a hero to her as other passengers join in to do what they can. When you are stopped at a light, let that car trying to turn right into your lane get in there. Let the person behind you in the grocery store who has just a few items go before you and your Mormon family cartful. Not only will they say, "Thank you," when you make the offer, watch how many times they say, "Thank you again," after they have been checked out. We have suppressed our inner goodness through detachment and busy-ness. That inner goodness requires a little coaxing through a mandatory daily assignment to bring it to the surface.

My transformation on thank-yous was so extensive that even when I have to write a letter or e-mail of correction or complaint, I begin with, "Thank you for all that you do to..." That tone of graciousness demands something lovely in the response. Responses come quickly because you began positively, with thanks for what they have done right or for their effort. Funny, that one of life's profound lessons would come to me from gravediggers. They do work their magic on recovery for the bereaved.

9

GREEN GRASS: WHEN PERMANENCE SETS IN

There are so many times during the first year following the sudden loss of a loved one that you live in denial. You wake up and begin the same routine that was your life before your loved one took the rapid transit to the hereafter. Claire was a special needs child, and, without fail, I rose each day at 4:30 a.m. to start her feeding pump. Claire had a feeding tube for almost twelve years of her life, and it had to be started no later than 4:45 a.m. or she could not get her formula and juice into her before the special short bus arrived to take her to school. On the weekends there was no sleeping in either. If a child eats at 4:45 a.m. five days per week, she becomes very vocal by 5:00 a.m. if the pump is not going.

Waking up at 4:30 a.m. for the better part of twenty years is a hard habit to break. I still don't need an alarm because 4:30 a.m. comes quite naturally to me. After Claire died, I had so many mornings where my feet hit the floor and headed right for Claire's room. In the fog of the wee hours, there I was cranking up the feeding pump. Then Claire's absence would hit, as would the tears. You want to turn back the clock. You want your old life back. You want your child.

Breaking those habits became a little bit easier because of the cemetery. There were marking points, literally and figuratively, that broke the painful patterns I kept assuming. When the Anna-suggested tin marker appeared on Claire's grave, there was a jolt. There was our daughter's name, date of birth, and date of death. Then came the permanent marker, complete with cement encasement and metal vase. We say it so often, that phrase, "Well, it's not carved in stone," that we forget it is the idiom of all idioms when it comes to permanence. Here was the essence of "carved in stone." Headstones, tombstones, and markers are one of the idiom's origins and refinements. "There's no turning back now," was my thought.

There is also the grass at the cemetery—it begins to grow in onto the dirt that covers the grave. You see it creeping slowly to cover the wound. Each day I saw new tendrils inching their way over Claire's grave. As they spread, they also began to fill in until there was less and less dirt. I remember the day the last patch of dirt was covered. "There's no turning back now," was the thought once again.

Grass is a metaphor for the healing. It creeps in, keeps stretching, and slowly covers up that wound in the middle of the serene meadows of the cemetery. There is a symbolism here—when the wound is covered, the grander picture and its serenity return. That awkward dirt is no longer there to mar the surface. The grave is no longer visible—it has become part of its surroundings. Grief works the same way—other things slowly cover it until it is no longer a surface mar in your life.

I know others see this symbolism. I noted in my cemetery visits that some grieving relatives bring sod straight away, so that they can cover the wound with instant grass. I've even seen some Astroturf here and there for those folks who want an NFL look. They are opting for the crash course in moving things along to permanence, hoping that when the wound is not so obvious that the pain will not be so great.

But in my year of living cemeterily, I witnessed one family that kept removing the grass. It has now been four years from the time their twelve-year-old son passed away, yet there is no grass on his grave. Each week, they turn back the grass, hack out those creeping tendrils, and restore the grave to its dirt finish. They do place some very uniform lines with a rake on the grave's dirt. But they want dirt and dirt only. No grass allowed. Of all the people I have met in the cemetery, they are the only ones who have shown no progress in their healing. It is as if they believe they can change things back if they can keep the grass from covering the grave. You can't. Nature marches on, with its defiant beauty and will have its way. Resisting her is a tall order that involves lots of weekly digging.

So it is with grief—the Spirit of the Comforter is there, slowly planting its seeds of reassurance and comfort. It is relentless because it is natural and it is a gift. Like the grass, it will have its way and it will cover the dirt. The wonderful thing is that, like the grass, the coverage of the wound is pretty, natural, and a slow process that accommodates our need to ease into the new look. There is no Astroturf for achieving the Comforter's solace, but the Comforter is a far too classy act to demand superficial healing. The Comforter wants the real thing for us and will work as slowly as the grass and its tendrils. And then one day you have the reality of permanence, but it is coupled with the beauty of healing. The grass in the cemetery taught me a great deal about the Comforter. President Thomas S.. Monson has taught, "Most of the time there are no flags waving or bands playing when prayer is answered. His miracles are frequently performed in a quiet and natural manner."[27] Sometimes the Comforter gives us our miracles in the way the tendrils of grace slowly embrace us and take root. It takes a cemetery to teach me that lesson.

10

THE BABY SECTION

When you have your first exposure to a cemetery, it is usually because a grandparent has passed away. Someone else made the funeral arrangements, and you just attend the services and burial. And, if you are young and impressionable, victimized by *The Sixth Sense* and *Tales of the Crypt*, you want nothing further to do with the layout, logistics, and patterns of the cemetery. But, hang around a cemetery long enough, and you realize that there is zoning, yes, even master plans.

Cemeteries have what is called a "baby section." The baby section of the cemetery is that section where the headstones are smaller and the graves are closer together, for obvious reasons. Tiny caskets don't need six feet of space. You also get a bargain on the plot and casket. Lose a child while she is still small and you save on funeral expenses. Crass commercialism creeps into all aspects of life and death.

The cemetery director had explained the baby section to us because our Claire was so tiny that she felt we might be better placing her in that section. However, her casket was larger than the maximum four feet permitted for the "baby section," so Claire went to sit at the big people's table in the cemetery. Still, her plot was in a new portion of the cemetery, near the baby section.

There is an immediately striking physical difference between what amounts to the Thanksgiving table division in the cemetery. There are the adult tables and the kid tables. They look different. And just like at Thanksgiving, the adult tables have different decorations. The baby section has balloons, stuffed animals, and toys on the headstones. There is even a warning sign from Rosencrantz and Guildenstern to leave the toys in the baby section alone. The sign is touching because R and G even explain that those toys have been left by family members and are important to them. Hands-off is the baby section policy. It is as if we are saying that those who have lost an infant or toddler cannot be expected to handle any more challenges and sadness.

Within a few days of Claire's funeral, and during one of my initial cemetery visits, I found myself drawn to that baby section. What drew me to the baby section was a strange feeling of peace, a heightened sense of purity that seems to hover over these tiny graves. The draw that came to me that day was strong, but despite that powerful force I felt that day and have experienced over my year of visits, I also have noticed that the baby section has fewer visitors than any other part of the cemetery.

I have put the pieces of the absence-of-visitors mystery together in hindsight. When I walked through the baby section for the first time, I realized that such an exercise and encounter are not for the fainthearted. Many of the headstones had dates of birth and dates of death as one and the same. Some headstones are for twins, with the first twin dying on the day of his birth and the other following soon thereafter, having stayed only a few days or weeks beyond the sibling who had shared companionship in the womb and but a few hours for their rest of earthly life.

There were the graves of three-year-olds whose pictures were part of their headstones. Tots with curls, tots by Christmas trees, tots on trikes, and all with smiles. What could have taken these cherubs?

Therein lies the answer to the question, "Why so few visitors for the baby section?" Too painful. Perhaps their parents and others in their lives were still searching for their own answers to "Why?" and the sight of a tiny grave was not part of paying respects but a reopening of the wounds.

I wish they had come to visit. What I learned from my walk through the baby section was gratitude. I cannot fathom the loss of a vibrant toddler. I at least had my child for nearly two decades.

The walk through the baby section brought me yet another lesson of the cemetery that would be repeated almost daily, as if multiplication tables were being drilled into me: no matter how bad we think we have it, others' pain is worse. We wouldn't take their sorrows, trials, and injustices on for a minute because our sorrow looks better. There is nothing quite like a feeling of superiority—"With my loss, I still didn't get hit as bad as you did"—to take you out of self-pity. I found myself repeating the David Letterman saying, "I wouldn't give your troubles to a monkey on a rock." I was never quite sure where Mr. Letterman got the saying or even sure if I understood it completely, but it always came to mind when I could see that another person's troubles were far worse than mine.

The realization that others have greater challenges pulls away the self-absorption that fuels grief. Satan gets to us during despair. In a devotional address at Brigham Young University in 1980, Elder Jeffrey Holland said, "I know of nothing Satan uses quite so cunningly or cleverly in his work on a young man or woman in your present circumstances. I speak of doubt—especially self-doubt—of discouragement, and of despair."[28] Your concern shifts from yourself to heartfelt feelings for other parents and their loss. You worry about them. You wonder if they have been able to get through the grief. You wonder if you might help. You wonder if they are coping. You worry that they too are searching for "Grief for Dummies." The cemetery allowed me to turn outward, to the stories of those around me. My cup runneth over with gratitude. I was forced to remove some pain to make room.

11

DON'T EVEN THINK ABOUT COMING OVER HERE!

About two weeks after we had buried our Claire, I was sitting near her grave, using the time as I usually did, to write in my journal. For those two weeks, I had remained very quiet and withdrawn during my visits to the cemetery. The reticence and shyness were strictly the products of self-preservation. I had trouble talking to anyone for weeks after Claire's death without bursting into tears. Inflicting my body sobs on a stranger at the cemetery seemed to be asking too much of that stranger.

I had noted that there had been a funeral that day in the baby section. A young man had returned and was reaching into a full shopping bag of stuffed animals and placing them one by one on this new grave. I felt his glance several times, but I avoided eye contact. After half an hour of ocular jousting, he walked toward me. I wanted to race for my car, but by that time he was between me and my car. I felt dread. "Don't even think of coming over here, buddy. I am in no condition to help anyone. In fact, I need people helping me!" He obviously could not read minds or panic in faces.

He soon stood next to me. I stood up and said simply, "I am so sorry." He still had tears. I joined him. Really it was no big deal to work into a cry at this point in my recovery. When they forgot my ketchup at the drive-through I was generally into a square-box-of-Kleenex crying jag. Then he spoke. The floodgates opened, both in words and tears. When his story emerged, I was ashamed of my actions in trying to avoid him.

His nephew, Alex, a vibrant tot of three, had been bitten by a mosquito and contracted encephalitis. Alex never really fully recovered. Six months after contracting the horrific disease, Alex would die in his mother's arms on a flight between San Diego and Phoenix. The plane would make an emergency landing in Yuma. Alex's mother, Rachel, had been traveling to Phoenix to live with her mother for a while to see if the dryer climate of our desert could help his health. Phoenix would instead be little Alex's final resting place.

I was crying, but for someone else, and thinking to myself, "Could there be any story worse than this one?" Here was the baby section lesson again, one that would be expounded upon many times in the coming months. You don't want others' sorrows to cope with because they are much worse than your own. But, there was one additional lesson here that opened more doors (gates?) in my cemetery visits. Never miss the chance to talk to another mourner in the cemetery. They are there for the same reasons: to reflect, to understand, to put issues to rest, to heal, and sometimes just to find someone who has some understanding of grief and its challenges. Indeed, generalize—never miss the time to talk to someone who reaches out to you. Talk, listen, ask, and realize that no matter your vulnerability, you are helping them.

James R. Talmage once noted, among all of his much noteworthy, "The Master associated love for God with love for fellowman; and surely love comprises duty, and duty means effort and action. A very large part of the course of education provided in the school of mortality is attained through association with our kind and the righteous observance of duty in community life. We are not here to be recluses nor to hold ourselves aloof from public service, but to live in a state of mutual helpfulness and effective cooperation."[29]

One of the risks of grief is aloofness. You miss a great deal of the course of study in the school of mortality when you become an island. That day I was schooled by a young man who missed his nephew. C. S. Lewis explained, "Grief is like a long valley, a winding valley where any bend may reveal a totally new landscape."[30] The landscape has an even greater chance of changing once you stop to talk to a fellow sojourner in the valley of grief.

12

I'M GLAD I'M NOT BACK
WHERE YOU ARE

our months after Claire died, a family buried their son in a plot very
close to Claire's. I happened to arrive that day just as the funeral was
ending. A young woman lingered after all the others who had been
there had gone their separate ways. Or perhaps they were off to the bizarre
postfuneral luncheon.

Like me in my early cemetery days, she avoided eye contact. As she
stood over the grave and my favorite Rosencrantz and Guildenstern covered
it, I had an epiphany: "I am so glad that I am not back where you are."
There was no feeling of smug superiority on this reaction. Rather, there was
the realization that with the passage of time, a mere four months, I could
see a difference between the way I was now and how unprepared, numb,
and lost I had been on the day of Claire's funeral. I could see that I had progressed and all because this young woman chose to linger.

I also realized that it was now incumbent on me, who found such a
dearth of resources for support during my initial grief, to reach out and
help. I did the ocular jousting this time, and when we made eye contact I
walked toward her and said, "I am so sorry." She was not able to offer much

except to say that it was her brother. It's a risky business to ask for details when teens and young adults are taken from this life. This young man was just a few months older than Claire when he died. There are car accidents, overdoses, and too many self-inflicted tragedies in this age group. I did not press but only offered, "I am here quite a bit. Your brother and my daughter were very close in age. Let me know if you need an ear or a shoulder."

In the years that have passed since that first encounter, I have seen this young woman many times. We hardly know each other, yet we do. I have never forgotten what her lingering after the funeral did for me that day. I don't know if I helped her. I just know there is always a tender look shared between us when we end up at the cemetery at the same time.

She taught me on that sad and dark day for her that I was getting better. The change in me is not the kind of change you notice immediately. The feelings of being "okay" fall over us slowly and gracefully. C. S. Lewis described his recovery: "There was no sudden, striking, and emotional transition. Like the warming of a room or the coming of daylight. When you first notice them they have already been going on for some time."[31]

Her anguish that day forced me to do something that does not come naturally—to reach out. I learned that I could do more than just speak when spoken to. I also learned that you can offer others the wisdom and insight time has brought to you in your journey with grief as a companion. I was the new Anna. When we are in the service of our fellow man, woman, sister, uncle, mother, grandparent, and any other living relative, our sorrows take a back seat.

13

MOTHER'S DAY

Just four months after Claire died I was facing Mother's Day. I had lost my mother one year and three days before Claire died. I hated the first Mother's Day after my mom died. I resented Hallmark and all their cards, in whatever format: merry, loving, angry, and sometimes in just darn bad taste. You find yourself standing in the Walgreen's card aisle, hands on hips, foot tapping, thinking, "How dare you! Do you not realize there are those of us who have no mothers?" Seattle won't let folks call tall fir trees in the public square in December "Christmas trees" for fear of offending those who don't celebrate the Savior's birth and the folks up there renamed Easter eggs "spring spheres" for fear of offending anyone who has not yet grasped the Resurrection. But where are these kinds of cranks when you want to banish Mother's Day? The month of May is filled with posters and ads that read, "Don't forget Mother's Day!" Who could? Especially when Mom has moved on to the next life.

But there was my saving grace on Mother's Day 2007. My mother was with Claire. Who better to be in charge if I couldn't be with my daughter? The only thing that gave me pause was that I worried those two were having a heck of a conversation about their DNA connector.

Claire: "I just hated all that yogurt she fed me before I got my feeding tube."

My mom: "Let me tell you something. She never heard of yogurt until she went off to college and had her head filled with highfalutin granola nonsense."

Claire: "And can you believe how she always had to have everything spotless in the house?"

My mom: "Oh, here's a dose of reality. Not once did she clean her room without threatened bodily injury. Dust bunnies bred like, well, rabbits under her bed."

I fell in love with the notion that Claire could complain to someone who would nod in agreement.

On Mother's Day I went to the cemetery early, thinking I would avoid the onslaught that Rosencrantz and Guildenstern warned me about. Mother's Day is the big cemetery holiday. Traffic jams, Mylar balloons floating and crisping in the wind, live flowers, new silk flowers, and tears abound on Hallmark's big day. Sadly, Veterans Day and Memorial Day don't come close.

But there is no avoiding the crowds at the cemetery on Mother's Day. At 7 a.m., opening time, they were there. Mom draws a crowd. Curiosity drew me back at noon that first Mother's Day after Claire died, and the crowds were still there. Mother's Day in Phoenix promises at least a hundred-degree day, but the cemetery was still full. This year I went to the cemetery at dusk on Mother's Day—no difference. There is something about the loss of a mother that never leaves us. In my many visits to the cemetery on Mother's Day, I have seen all types of folks there to pay tribute to Mom. Some come in BMWs, some in dilapidated Cutlasses, and some come in large groups on motorcycles, boasting more tattoos than skin. Somehow you know that the world will be fine when you see a big lug in railroad boots and a do-rag lean over a grave and place a rose.

That first Mother's Day in the cemetery as I sat and watched the children of so many moms pay tribute, I envisioned moms looking down at the cemetery on Mother's Day and muttering, "Sure, now you visit!" I thought also that perhaps if I listened carefully I could hear their subtle whispers of advice: "And get a haircut."

The quiet reflection of my cemetery brought home the unchangeable reality of the irreplaceable role that mothers play. No one leaves the same indelible impression that a mother does on a life. The ties that bind defy the departure death brings. I felt gratitude for the insight that Mother's

Day works on both sides of the veil. Claire was looking down on me in the cemetery and whispering, "I love you, Mom." There in the cemetery that first Mother's Day I spoke back. I said, ever so softly as I stood by Claire's grave, "I love you too, Sweet Pea," and my mom standing by with her wisdom as she assured, "See, you are both just fine!"

14

WE REALLY DO GRIEVE IN DIFFERENT WAYS

I've heard it so many times, "Everyone grieves in their own way." Everyone says it, but no one really believes it. We have our framework for grieving, and when others cross our self-imposed lines of propriety we conclude they really were not that sad. You are walking through the valley of the shadow of death, and people who spout, "Everyone grieves differently," are the first to question you, "Do you think that's really good for you?" Only those who have not grieved have such low tolerance levels for grief behavior. In my year at the cemetery I have seen the human condition in grieving and all its varieties.

Near to our Claire's grave is the grave of a twelve-year-old boy, the grassless one. The headstone is covered with Matchbox trucks and cars, food, candles, toys, photos, and, thanks to these choices in commemoration, ants. Each Monday evening, and many others in between, an extended family of about thirty-seven people, complete with a caravan of vans, cars, and toddlers, descends on the grave. Plastic chairs encircle the grave of this young man, a grave that would remain, in all its glory, just dirt. They always held a picnic at their son's grave. Why not? The ants had already arrived.

During the summer months when the Phoenix sun was setting they would erect an Army- green umbrella so large that it could house a special forces unit. Their shade from a brutal western sunset.

Not once did I see a tear shed. They made me crazy. "Respect for the dead!" "Respect for the dead!" was all I kept muttering under my breath. On more than one occasion in my early months of grief, I chastised the running urchins about being quiet. This was my daughter's grave and here were the Joads setting up camp.

I began visiting the cemetery at a time on Mondays that allowed me to avoid the traveling Wilburys and their barbecue. For almost a year I made no eye contact. I worried that I would launch into them with a tirade about impropriety. Each time I accidentally ran into their carnival by the grave, I bit my tongue so hard that I drew blood a few times.

One Monday night I realized that they had been coming to the cemetery for one year, just as I had. I glanced over at them and there was an odd moment of silence as they all looked at the photo of their now departed happy lad. My heart hurt because I was ashamed. Their pain was as real as mine, but their approach to grief brought out the worst in me—I had been judgmental.

I needed to make it right, so I walked over and said, "Mi Español es muy malo." And it is. They all smiled, not really quite sure what to do with their bilingual Grinch who had glared at them for over a year. I added, "¿Tu hijo?" One of them said, "Si." I could only say, "Lo siento." I had no more to offer, my Spanish being what it is, except "Tengo catarro," not because I had a cold but because that's only one of two things I could remember at that moment. Also, from my days of teaching Spanish kindergarten when I could actually generate the language, "Sientese!" came to mind. But they already had their chairs set up and were firmly planted. Awkward nonbilingual silence. Then from the van came a young woman who said, "I speak English." We smiled. We spoke. We talked of the amazing healing properties of the cemetery. We had both long noted each other but never spoken. I was sad to have lost out on their warmth and comfort for so long. They are charming, caring people who lost a son.

We grieve in different ways, or do we? I'm not one for egg salad and chips at the graveside, but they were. We had all discovered the same miracle cure for dealing with the grief of losing a child. We were one in both loss and recovery. I had done nothing to help them because our grieving process was different. Yes, the process is different. But grief is the same. They had lost a son. I had lost a daughter. We both lost them too soon, and we understood each other. Language barriers are largely irrelevant when it comes to love extended to help with grief. It just took me over a year to figure it out.

I find myself more often than not at the cemetery on Monday nights—for the picnic. Sometimes the woman who speaks English is not there. It doesn't matter. We wave. We smile. And I bought Rosetta Stone for Spanish. I need to learn some grief words in Spanish.

15

THERE ARE NO ATHEISTS IN GRAVEYARDS

Early on in my daily cemetery ventures I had a revelation. There are no atheists in graveyards. There are those outside cemeteries who talk a good game about there being no God or who express their disdain for organized religion. Christopher Hitchens, before his death, turned a violent phrase when speaking of the dangers of organized religion, and even unorganized faiths. The faith that Madonna subscribes to doesn't seem to have much order to it except the obligatory red bracelet and what seem to be yoga classes. Grateful Dead groupies and roadies have more structure in their devotion. Deadheads are a pretty reverent lot, something that may just be a function of middle age setting in.

Like so many outside the cemetery, Christopher Hitchens hated the simplicity, the dogma, the zeal, and the imagined dangers of religion. In fact, Mr. Hitchens said that the one thing he learned from religion is "the complete ephemerality of human power, and human existence—the transience of all states, empires, heroes, grandiose claims, and so forth."[32] Apart from his clear understanding that the Lord is no respecter of persons, Hitchens sounded misguided and morose, a real barrel of laughs.

My friends at the cemetery who have just lost loved ones are more upbeat. Every conversation in the cemetery finds my confidants working in the following: "I know they are fine and live on," or "They are with God now." In the hundreds of conversations with grieving relatives that I have had at the cemetery over the course of my 365 days, give or take 365 more, I never found one who denied either the existence of God or an afterlife. The phraseology is different, but the faith is there. I noted a quote in the *New York Times* from Gwendolen Greene, the cousin of Lashanda Armstrong, a young mother who drove her minivan into the Hudson River, killing herself and three of her children, ages five years, two years, and eleven months. Ms. Greene said, poignantly, "We lost them, but I know God's going to take them."[33] She offered her thoughts as she looked at the caskets of the three tiny children.

There are few atheists at funerals either—faith emerges in losses and the inexplicable. In the humility of loss and grief, we find our way to faith. The headstone of former Ohio State head football coach Woody Hayes has the following engraved on it, "And in the night of death, hope sees a star, and listening love hears the rustle of a wing." Ironically, that's Robert C. Ingersoll's line from a eulogy he wrote for his brother. Ingersoll, a very vocal and dedicated atheist, found himself questioning, wondering, and worrying when he faced the loss of his brother. That head-turner of a phrase came to us from an atheist because he was trying to cope with the loss of his brother.

Sometimes the loss of a loved one is the first time those whose arrogance found them immune from religion's rigors are forced to explore the meaning of life. Sometimes the death is so sudden and the taking so unjust, that they are forced to believe that there is a greater purpose, a life beyond this one, and another chance for them. Grief without the promise of eternal life asks too much, even of an atheist. They find their comfort in their own newfound faith or they rely on what they have heard others say. But there are no mourners in a cemetery who can't have a good discussion on God, grace, and the next life.

When God gives us more than we can handle alone, we turn to Him. I wonder if our loved ones are aware of the gift their passing bestows on those they left behind? Grief has its sobering qualities. But in my year of cemetery experiences I learned that grief also has the ability to foster faith. It fosters faith, and faith fosters strength. Strength allows recovery. And with this sequence of traits we have the full explanation for why there are no atheists in graveyards. There are no atheists in foxholes because of fear. There are no atheists in graveyards because of unanswered questions. The loss of a loved one demands exploration of the human condition, our role, and what we really want out of life. What we really want, and loss brings it home, is the next life. Another life requires a Divine Being. Those hanging around cemeteries feel Him acutely. They do so because they need Him.

I suspect Christopher Hitchens might have slipped into W. C. Fields mode just prior to his death. Known for his similar hatred of religion, Fields found religion near the end of his life. A friend who was visiting Fields at the hospital found the great comedian in his bed reading the Bible. When asked by the much-surprised friend what he was doing, Fields replied, "Looking for loopholes." Death brings regrets to the atheist. But grief gives us survivors a second chance to immerse ourselves in faith and begin anew our course for renewal of covenants. Claire's passing renewed my faith—it was her last gift to me.

16

ANGELS WITH SENSES OF HUMOR

In the first few months after Claire died, body sobs did kick in as I stood or sat by Claire's grave. Some days were bad. The remaining days were worse. I went nine months before I didn't cry each day. Kicking the funk of those tears was a challenge. I believe I had help. Oddly, the help came through humor.

I actually had noticed this phenomenon of assistance through laughs when I lost my mother. Prior to her death, my mother had been ill for nearly two years. My parents lived out of state, and I managed to travel there about once each month for that time. I now treasure those times that I had on those weekends to be of some small help to her and my father.

Days before my mother died, my children and I had been to visit my parents for the holidays, and my mother, while in a special care center because she was intubated, seemed to be doing better. After the holidays, the family all disbanded, comfortable that she was stable. I headed to Chicago to give a speech. When I landed there were just too many messages on my phone to come from a void in cell phone connection during a late-evening evening flight. I knew something was wrong, and I knew exactly what it was.

Without listening to the messages, I called Terry, and he broke the news to me that my mother had died. Because my flight was late, it was well past midnight. The Chicago airport was eerily empty. I sat down at one of the gates and cried. The passengers from my flight filed by, and still I sat. No flights out that night—no way to get back. Everyone had to leave the airport. Even the TSA folks were long gone. I caught a cab to get to the hotel and spend the night before returning. I was visibly shaken and upset. My cab driver, someone from a Krakhozia-type nation, was, bless him, concerned.[34] He asked if I was "okay." I explained that I had just received the news that my mother had just died. He was beside himself and hardly knew what to say, but he managed some way to express his empathy: "How about a cigarette?"

It was an ironic offering for his Mormon passenger. But, from my dear new friend, this was a sincere and caring offer. His humble offer was tender and, well, funny. I had to laugh. This terrific offering saw me through a tough few hours. In fact, when I called my dad from the hotel, I shared the story with him. Although he had just lost his wife of fifty-six years, he could not help but have his heart lifted.

Because of that experience I had to pause in wonder. Is it possible that those around us are prompted to say things that help us? Or, is it possible that they are placed there because of their nature and how they would be the ideal individual to help at a time of need? I had no answers for these questions, and we may not find out until the next life. But something that occurred to me in that cab in Chicago would reemerge on a regular basis during my year at the cemetery. I have been given the blessings of well-placed humorists and serendipity that are sent to me at my times of greatest need. The frequency of these angels from among us who are comedians—Emmy-potential comedic writers they are—and come my way has led me to conclude that mere chance is not responsible for the smiles and comfort they have given to me.

We are cautioned in Section 88 of the Doctrine and Covenants about laughter, and the warnings on laughter are grouped in verse 121 with similar warnings about "pride" and "lustful desires."[35] Our prophets have all demonstrated delightful senses of humor, and President Hinckley counseled us to get some humor: "We've got to have a little humor in our lives. You had better take seriously that which should be taken seriously but, at the same time, we can bring in a touch of humor now and again. If the time ever comes when we can't smile at ourselves, it will be a sad time." President Hinckley was offering the same cautions on laughter, but in the context of other scripture, "A merry heart doeth good, like medicine."[36]

Laughter is medicine for grief. I would not have picked this particular remedy for seeing through my grief, but I believe it was chosen for me because the Lord knew there was a receptive heart for humor. Laughter through tears provided the emotional boost that saw me through the rugged territory of the grieving process.

17

MICHAEL CORLEONE AND HIS OLDS NEED DIRECTIONS

The humor stories from my one year plus of experience are as varied as the people I met. There was one day as I stood by Claire's grave that was a particularly difficult one for me—full-body sobs that day. Whilst I was wallowing in my tears, a car came careening around the bend near Claire's resting place. The car almost made the turn on two wheels. And what a car! It was one of those nondescript, long, long, Oldsmobiles, bordering on gunboat size. Of course, the Olds was that root beer Popsicle brown that was so popular in the 1970s, and this car's splendor was only improved by its peeling vinyl roof. The driver had slicked-back hair that could have given him a bodyguard role in *The Godfather*. An added bonus was his Ari Onassis/Anthony Quinn black-framed glasses. He had on a white T-shirt. He slammed on his brakes—the windows in his car were already down. I believe they were down out of disrepair, not choice. He yelled across two hundred feet to me in an accent that was a combination of a Chicago Bears fan and a New Jersey teamster, "Where's the office?"

I directed him, and, with no acknowledgment or thanks, he put his lead foot to the pedal and sped over to the cemetery office. That poor delicate woman in charge of the cemetery office who always speaks in her librarian voice was in for a treat. A chuckle came. Sometimes I think I was hallucinating when I saw these characters for they seemed to have Dan Aykroyd tendencies and had walked off a *Saturday Night Live* set to help me at the cemetery. Thank you, Providence, for the help with the tears.

Brad Wilcox's article "If You Can Laugh at It, You Can Live with It" was an inspiration to me during this time. One quote from his article sums up what my serendipity humorists were bringing. "President Hugh B. Brown (1883–1975), a counselor in the First Presidency, recognized the value of facing challenges with humor: 'A wholesome sense of humor will be a safety valve that will enable you to apply the lighter touch to heavy problems and to learn some lessons in problem solving that "sweat and tears" often fail to dissolve.'"[37]

When Satan was drawing me in with his lulling reassurance that my inability to recover was because of the injustices I was handed and the sobs would start, I got the blessing of humor handed to me in the cemetery. I had felt the Comforter many times, but I came to realize that the Comforter has different techniques for helping us cope. Sometimes they arrive in a brown Delta 88.

18

THE UNICYCLIST

On still another worst-of-the-bad-days, I was leaving the cemetery in body-sob tears. I stopped at the exit to check for traffic. What I saw made me believe that I really did have grief problems, that I had slipped into hallucinations, and was in bad need of counseling. There was a very thin young man wearing straight-leg Levis with no belt. He also had a magnificent mullet hairdo and was riding a unicycle. Truly, how often do you see that at the cemetery? In fact, how often in your life have you seen a man with a mullet riding a unicycle? In fact, who would dream up putting unicycle and mullet in the same sentence?

Heaven was pulling out all the stops for me—sending the equivalent of three-ring circuses my way to cheer me up. The best part of this story was the confirmation that I was not hallucinating. A woman had pulled up next to my car and was waiting to make her right turn. As Mullet Man wheeled past me, my head turned toward her car. She then turned her head toward my car as if we were passing the baton in a relay. Her eyes followed him as he crossed in front of her car, and then we both sat, dazed at what had cycled into our cemetery lives. We looked at each other, shrugged, and smiled. I'm just glad I had a witness for this angelic comedic visitation.

There's a trick to this humor therapy. You have to be willing to see the gifts you are given. Once I had been through the cab driver, the Olds, and now Mullet Man, I noticed a change in me. Inward focus shifted to observation. Truth be told, I became anxious to see what gift of humor I would be given as I chugged through my grief.

I was working at achieving the balance between the serious issues of life and its joy. Jeffrey Holland, in a talk on the taking and administration of the Sacrament, spoke of the need for good cheer, "We could remember that even with such a solemn mission given to him, the Savior found delight in living; he enjoyed people and told his disciples to be of good cheer. He said we should be as thrilled with the gospel as one who had found a great treasure, a veritable pearl of great price, right on our own doorstep. We could remember that Jesus found special joy and happiness in children and said all of us should be more like them—guileless and pure, quick to laugh and to love and to forgive, slow to remember any offense."[38]

I had been missing the good cheer part of the gospel—my humorists were guiding me back to it.

19

THE TESTIMONIES WHEN ALL IS WELL

For every parent who loses a child, there will be ten who have a healthy child who will live to collect Social Security (if the economy holds out). For every Mormon mother who loses a child, testimony meetings during that first year will be difficult. I listened during that first year following my mother's death and again following Claire's death as members described how their testimony was increased because a parent recovered, a child was diagnosed and treated just in time, or how Heavenly Father answered their prayers for healing their children. I remained grateful for their testimonies and know that they were strengthened by the positive outcomes of their experiences. But, their testimonies were grounded in the fact that all's well that ends well. As a mother who had lost a child and her mother, I couldn't help but wonder why their prayers were answered in the way they wanted, but mine were not. I would then move to more negative territory and think, "Let's see how you do when the outcome is not so good."

There was testimony meeting just months after Claire's death when a parent was describing an accident involving his daughter. He detailed vividly how his daughter could not breathe and how she was turning blue and gasping. Having watched our Claire's last breaths, the description was too much to bear. His daughter was saved, but mine was not. Worse, I did not want to relive Claire's passing. Witnessing the moment of death is an experience that holds a grip on the mind forever. The goal is to keep it from erupting too often. And here I was in testimony meeting, being forced to relive it.

During testimonies such as these, I had to curb feelings of resentment and rushes of cynicism even as I wondered whether our Heavenly Father was really there with me. Walking out was my first defense mechanism. I would walk out and go to the cemetery. But, if you know the nature of testimonies in our testimony meetings, that strategy will render you inactive. And don't forget that all testimonies are preceded by the blessing of babies. Tradition brings the testimonies of mother and father and their gratitude for this new life. Ouch! The great walkout ploy was not serving me nor my testimony well.

On my last testimony walkout, as I stood by Claire's grave, I had an epiphany. Surely someone else understands that some testimonies are difficult for members to hear and do little to help. Indeed, some testimonies just hurt. Such an insight seemed to run contra to personal revelation. In effect, I was asking, "Have any of the general authorities ever given us counsel on mean testimonies?" Turns out, they had! Well, general authorities that they are, they were not as "way harsh," as my kids would say, on the topic. However, I sought help, and I found it. President Kimball reminded us not to preach and to stay focused on the knowledge we have that has been given through the power of the Holy Ghost.[39] Dallin Oaks counseled us in 2008, "A testimony of the gospel is not a travelogue, a health log, or an expression of love for family members."[40]

During those two years of testimony meetings (once I quit walking out), I developed a strong testimony of the counsel we have received about what we say in testimony meetings. I had a seismic change in both my understanding of and attitude toward testimony meeting. The change came from the combination of the counsel from our leaders as well as my heightened sensitivity to the differing circumstances of our brothers and sisters in the ward. When we talk about our wonderful spouses in a testimony, we salt the wounds of those who are going through or have been through a painful divorce. When we share our experiences on a cross-country trip we fail to realize that there are those whose economic status or personal circumstances (caring for an ill family member at home) will never allow them to have your experiences. But, when we speak about a scripture we have pondered, an insight we have gained, and offer our certainty about the atonement, we are on common ground. Regardless of what life has handed our brothers and sisters, they can all read the scriptures, study, and come to understand what you are testifying to. Testimonies should be common ground, not one-upmanship on trials or the seeking of attention.

I had missed all of the counsel of our leaders on testimonies. I had lost sight of the purpose of bearing our testimonies. Had I not felt the pain of the travelogues, health logs, and so on that were part of so many testimonies, I would not have developed the understanding of their purpose as well as the sensitivity to stay on common ground when bearing my own testimony.

20

THE PURPLE SUBURBAN WITH FLAMES

In that last testimony meeting before I ended my walkouts, my walkout was triggered by that young father who was explaining a serious injury to one of his children and how frightened he was as he saw his child stop breathing. The sight of your child not being able to breathe was something that was just too painful for me to revisit. This dear young father meant no harm. How could he know? But, the tears just flowed. So, the walkout came. With the rest of the family out of town, I had only my youngest son with me. I turned to him and explained that we needed to leave. He was confused, but he took the cue (and the break from church) very well. Once we had made it out of the church, the body sobs set in. My poor little guy didn't know what to do except hold my hand.

Our church building is within walking distance from our home. Together, my cherished youngest and I walked to our gate on the south side of our neighborhood. I sobbed. He watched me but clearly did not know what to say. When we got to the gate, I saw something that forced me to ask my young son whether I was hallucinating through my tears. I queried him carefully (not wanting to reveal the insanity card if that's indeed what was happening), "Do you see what I see?" And he responded, "You mean the low-rider Chevy Suburban painted metallic purple with orange, red, and yellow flames along the bottom?" That will stop your tears. All I could say was, "Now there's something you don't see every day."

So convinced was I that he was hallucinating this comedic moment with me that I told him we needed to rush home and get a camera. "But, Mom," he said, "There's no chance it will still be here by the time we get back." We rushed with hope. The purple flame wagon was using the intercom trying to gain access to the neighborhood, and I responded, "John, don't be so negative! I know the board members for the HOA. They have probably put deed restrictions against this kind of car in our neighborhood. Whoever is in that Suburban will be negotiating for hours to get in."

Either the screening process had its flaws or the purple flame wagon gave up, but John and I failed in our quest for photographic evidence of the car that broke my sobs. Even if it was a hallucination, I am grateful for the spurring of the imagination that gave me relief from a moment that was bringing back far too much pain from Claire's passing. John still brings it up, "Hey, Mom, remember when we saw that purple Suburban with the flames?" I do, and we both smile.

Perhaps it was a Suburban full of angels, but I am not sure a purple-flamed ride would be the choice of cherubim. Apart from another one of my comedic moments, I learned another tool for grief. I have great detail on my year of living cemeterily because I was keeping a journal. I did not want to forget how—and how much—I was helped along the way. I did not want to forget the lessons I was being taught—I love to learn. It's the being taught that was bothering me, as one of my colleagues says. For some people these experiences would have rolled by as insignificant events. For me, because I was keeping a journal of the cemetery and my recovery, the stories were recorded. Whimsy is also an antidote for grief.

Auntie Mame said life was a banquet and most of us are starving because we miss what's being offered. I was given the bounteous blessing of a buffet of characters sent my way to help me through some rough waters. Norman Cousins, a sort of Renaissance man who was a journalist, editor, and adjunct professor at UCLA's medical school, studied the biochemistry of human emotions. Later in his life, he put his research to work, research that found a connection between laughter and reduction in pain. As he suffered from either Marie-Strümpell disease or reactive arthritis (there is some disagreement), he discovered the pain-reducing effects of watching Marx Brothers movies: "I made the joyous discovery that ten minutes of genuine belly laughter had an anesthetic effect and would give me at least two hours of pain-free sleep. When the pain-killing effect of the laughter wore off, we would switch on the motion picture projector again and not infrequently, it would lead to another pain-free interval."[41] He wrote *Anatomy of an Illness as Perceived by the Patient: Reflections on Healing*, the book on humor's role in speeding and facilitating recovery from illness.[42] Grief is a type of emotional illness, and certainly biochemistry is in play. I like to think that Mr. Cousins would welcome the application of his theory to my recovery. Mr. Cousins's humor was the simplest and purest type: Marx Brothers madcap and physical comedy—the type of humor in which there is no ill will or suggestive nature. All the characters sent my way were possessed of that purest of humor.

I reached a point at which I used my grief medicine to help others. One afternoon at the cemetery, I was speaking with a grandmother who had lost a grandchild. She was distraught. I was doing my best to help. There was a funeral just finishing at the time we were talking. When she was at her saddest, one of the cars in the funeral procession wanted to leave and another car was in the way. The driver who wanted to leave laid on the horn and let loose with a string of obscenities that was shaking the cedars as if *NOTLD* ghouls were rattling about. The other driver honked back and a battle ensued. A friend or relative finally came and calmed the two drivers down before they exchanged gunfire. We looked at each other and I said, "Now there's something you don't see every day: road rage at a funeral." She laughed and said, "You're funny." I corrected her—it's the comedy writers in Heaven doing the heavy lifting on humor. I just record the stories; I don't write them.

21

MUST BE A SMALL CLASS

Another Rosencrantz and Guildenstern story has become one that I have used in many speeches. It is a story that is universally well received. I get the credit as a speaker, but I owe my dear gravediggers for their insight. I had stopped at Claire's grave on my way to work one day, and two of the city employees were nearby working to perfect the sprinkler timing for the grass. They approached me because by this time I was a clear regular and they seemed to be comfortable being around me. While they knew the story of Claire, they knew very little about me, and this day curiosity took over. As they approached, they asked if I was on my way to work. I said that I was. Rosencrantz and Guildenstern and I were far enough along in our relationship that they had some comfort in finding out more about me.

One asked, "What do you do?"

I have been hesitant to explain my exact occupation of being a professor of business ethics since the time of the Enron scandal because so many times I am met with a joke about the sheer futility of my line of work. Your self-esteem does suffer after enough jokes about your field. I answer questions about my work forthrightly, without giving up too much information. I was not forthcoming in response to my dear Rosencrantz and Guildenstern. I offered only, "I teach."

Brevity may be the soul of wit, but it was not enough for them, so they pushed. "Where do you teach?"

I explained, "I teach at ASU."

They were relentless and wanted more still. "What do you teach?"

I had to confess, "I teach business ethics."

They both paused for a moment, and then one said, "Must be a small class."

The wit was so clever and the insight such a head-turner that it took me a minute to catch up with him. Quite a zinger leveled on my oxymoronic field. Given the behavior of businesspeople over the past decade, he was right. Bless them. Bless the comedic angels. Bless Claire for bringing and/or sending them into my life. Who would have thought one-liners are available in the cemetery?

22

THE CLEAN SWEEP: A SIX-MONTH CLEANUP

Without fail, every January and July bring the six-month cleanup. Rosencrantz and Guildenstern put up white placards at both entrances of the cemetery to give us warning. On January 15 and July 15, the placards seem to shout, "Folks, we're cleaning up the place." Under the cemetery rules, anything other than the flowers in the vases that are part of the headstones must go. The Bud Lights, the Marlboros, the trucks, the stuffed animals, the food items that adorn the graves—they are slated for the dump.

And what a collection it is—this semiannual roundup of tributes. People grieve in different ways, and they pay their respects with an even greater range of options. Most of us choose flowers. Some choose tobacco and liquor. The Japanese at least have the good sense to pay tribute with a healthy meal offering to their departed love ones. But in the United States, if beer made Milwaukee famous, imagine what it can do for a departed love one. "This Bud's for you" is an ad slogan that has made its way into the grieving process.

The clean sweep is a magnificent process to behold. The clean sweep restores equality and uniformity to the cemetery. No longer are graves distinguished by their trappings—there's an egalitarianism to all graves with flowers only. It's as if Rosencrantz and Guildenstern understand the plan of salvation and are getting the terrestrial world ready. The Lord is no respecter of persons.[43] We might as well get used to the notion that we can't dress up the basics and hope to distinguish ourselves. What's on the grave is irrelevant. It's the spirit that counts.

There is also a beauty to cleanliness. I gained new appreciation for why it is next to Godliness.[44] Professor Katie Liljenquist of BYU's Marriott School of Management has established a connection between cleanliness and righteous behavior with her research. Employees are more ethical if their workplace smells better.[45] We live on a higher plane when we are in a clean atmosphere. A clean cemetery is a spiritual cemetery.

The cemetery sweep is akin to cleaning a closet, removing the clutter from the floor, and having the clothes hanging neatly and uniformly. You feel better, the clothes look better, they hang better, and you can find things. Those results of closet cleaning translate directly across to the cemetery. Visitors feel better, our departed ones are probably feeling more spiritual in this respectful environment, and we can find the graves more easily without all the clutter. While I have come to appreciate the unique decorations the loved ones of the dearly departed deposit, I also marvel in the dignity of equality and simplicity.

The clean sweep also brought home another realization: we cannot escape the cemetery. At some point in our lives, and most assuredly at the end, we will spend time at a cemetery or two. Hopefully, we will not occupy more than one cemetery in our passing, or those *NOTLD*/"Thriller" things will clearly have been correct in their assessment of dancing and/or migrating ghouls. But there is even egalitarianism in our departure from this life. The earthly remains do rest in similar places.

Cemetery decorations seem to be yet another way we try to use "stuff" (material goods) to put ourselves a step above the crowd. We even try to introduce a class system into the cemetery through decorations. We attempt to distinguish our dearly departed through more flowers, more memorabilia, more carvings on the headstone. More, more, more. Bigger, bigger, bigger. Oddly, however, the most distinctive graves, once the clean-sweep look dissipates with time as the clutter moves in and takes over, are those graves that are neat and simple. The simple graves are distinct because when you read the headstone and the "Born" and "Died" dates, your imagination runs wild. You perform all sorts of mathematical functions. "Ah, she was ten years younger than her husband," "She was born the day after my birthday," "The husband passed away one month after his wife died," and "They were only married for one year before she died." Mystery does bring dignity.

When the clutter, which begins to look weatherworn in the shortest time in the Arizona sun, rests on a grave it loses its mystery. When there is no clutter, you want to know more. You find yourself focusing on their life events, not the superficial decorations that will fade with the elements and find their way into the trash bins on clean-sweep day. Oh, how symbolic the cemetery decorations and their fading glory are! They are blown away, are swept away, or just have a faded look—"…for dust thou are, and unto dust shalt thou return…"[46] So, it is with all the "stuff" we acquire. What remains, when all the stuff of our lives is swept away, is our life. That record, that Book of Life, does not document stuff; it documents what we cannot see. "…the books were opened; and another book was opened, which was the book of life; but the dead were judged out of those things which were written in the books, according to their works…"[47]

I have also come to believe that those who have gone on to the next part of life's journey are not concerned about pretense. They don't want the tallest Christmas tree, the most solar lights, or even the Skoal can on their graves. They want us to learn to appreciate them for what they were—they want us to catch a glimpse of their Book of life. Somehow I believe our loved ones worry when we are decorating instead of meditating. I disembarked straight away from the "Best Decorated Grave" competition with its pretense and distraction once I witnessed the first clean sweep. I found peace in surrendering to simplicity in the cemetery. More important, the cemetery's lesson of simplicity's elegance carried over into life outside the cemetery.

The loss of one so close makes you realize that your life was filled with a great deal of attention-getting lights, buzzers, food, decorations, and just general busy-ness. Minimalist lives are as good as minimalist graves. In the year following Claire's death, the signal from the cemetery was an important one for reform, a reform of downsizing. I found myself buying less "stuff": fewer clothes, fewer decorations, fewer shoes, and, even, fewer snacks. Then I began taking the time to sort through existing "stuff" and ask, "Is this really necessary?" Most of it was not. By the end of the year, I no longer had a storage locker. I realized that I was paying monthly rent to store "stuff" I did not even remember was there. I cleaned out everything from closets to glove compartments to the space beneath the barbecue. It is a fabulous feeling to have empty shelves and no need to ask, "Where is...?" When you have a little bit of stuff, you know where that little bit is.

In her death, Claire was still teaching me. I found during this year of cemetery decoration observations that stuff lost its charm and draw. "Stuff" is the casual term for what results from materialism. I didn't stop at cleaning out stuff and giving away what was really not used. I began cleaning house financially, literally, and figuratively. We paid off the mortgage on our house. We still used credit cards, but only for the beloved Nordstrom points to "purchase" the kids' shoes or to get cash back. We paid off the cards each month. I found a simpler life away from materialism, a life that has its dignity.

Clean sweeps, which are so good for cemeteries, also work on houses, cars, offices, and financial portfolios. Eventually, the clean sweeps carry over into the soul. There's something about simplicity that is healing and good. Cleanliness is indeed next to Godliness, and right there with Godliness is the healing help for grief. The cemetery helped me get off the "stuff" train.

Frankly speaking, grief began to seem like a lot simpler task by contrast to the tall order of parting with our precious stuff. You can't serve God and Mammon.[48] I used to read the story of the young rich man who said he kept the commandments and wanted to know what he had to do in order to achieve eternal life. The Savior instructed him to sell everything he owned and follow the Savior. What I used to take away from the story is that he couldn't give up his money. But, the Savior chose his words carefully. He didn't say give up all your money; He said get rid of your stuff: "And he was sad at that saying, and went away grieved: for he had great possessions."[49] It's not the wealth that was the problem; the young man's problem was that he wanted the stuff for purposes of pride, rank, privilege. He was wedded to his stuff. Treasures on earth versus treasures in Heaven. "For where your treasure is, there will your heart be also."[50] It takes a cemetery full of junky decorations seen in contrast to the simplicity of the minimalist grave to help you grasp what the Savior taught.

23

ALICIA

Within a month following Claire's funeral, my daily visit to her grave found two women overwrought at a nearby grave. There were not just tears flowing. I sensed anger percolating. Because I had learned to reach out, I approached the two women. One, a woman named Grace, pointed to a grave and said, "That's my daughter. I don't think anyone cares now that she is gone." I realized that for the first time since I began hanging around a cemetery that there was some value in intelligence on graveyard visits. I could help someone else with the seemingly useless data I had been gathering via observation. I protested and reassured, "Oh, no! You are so wrong. I come each day, and I see young people here all the time, just sitting by her grave. It is rare for me to not see someone at her graveside." I am not a hugging person by nature, but Grace needed a hug. What an odd thing for me, veins flowing with British, Irish, Hungarian, stiff-upper-lip blood, to be doing! Hugging? No one in my ancestry hugs. You get that combination of DNA nationality and you have a sturdy, broad-shouldered, porch-sweeping, memo-writing piece of work. We toil, we save, we clean, and we serve meals on time. That's love. Who needs hugging as long as the floor is scrubbed?

Yet here I was in the cemetery hugging someone I had known for only five minutes. But then again, no one is ever really alone in a cemetery.

And those who you meet in the cemetery know a bit more about you at that point than your close friends because they have lived through your experience. They have lost someone, and they know the pain. My cemetery friends are now the friends of a lifetime. We hug all the time.

Following the hug and the reassurance of visitors, Grace's countenance changed; she thanked me. I had enough cemetery experience to know that she needed to talk. I knew from the headstone that her daughter was young, so I asked what happened.

As cemetery stories go, the story of Grace's daughter, Alicia, is one that tugs at my heart too much. Alicia was a twenty-nine-year-old successful young woman who had always been active in her church, chaste before marriage, and loyal to her husband after their marriage. They had been high school sweethearts. "Love of a lifetime," Grace said of Alicia's Steve.

Alicia had been on her way home from work on Christmas Eve when a truck passed her in her small car but didn't quite stay in his lane. Alicia's small car was taken under the truck. Alicia made it to the trauma unit, but with no hope. She passed away quickly. Grace and Steve complied with Alicia's wishes and allowed her organs to be taken. Alicia died on Christmas Day. Alicia was expecting her first child.

Alicia's death was unexpected and *prima facie* evidence of the old adage, "Only the good die young." Her mother struggled with the loss. Alicia and Steve had lived with her as they built their house. Of all the people I met in those first few months, Grace was the saddest. Her sadness was not for a lack of faith—she was a diligent churchgoer and listened to Christian music in her little white pickup.

I came to know and love Grace, a talented seamstress who made costumes, gowns, and tailoring. But she struggled because she knew that her Alicia was a gem of a child and a magnificent spirit of our Heavenly Father. Grace was one of my most frequent contacts at the cemetery. We seemed to run into each other more often than not despite work schedules that were varied and hectic. With each day Grace had another Alicia story. All the stories pointed to one inescapable conclusion: there was something about Alicia that was too good for this world.

The too-soon nature of Alicia's death bothered Grace. But Grace was also not permitted what now seemed to me to be my relatively simple process of allowing time to heal the grief. Her grief did not pass naturally because she seemed to experience ongoing drama surrounding her Alicia.

Her son-in-law married Alicia's best friend just a little over five months following Alicia's funeral. As we used to say in days gone by, "They had to get married," which was something we said because men who got women pregnant were expected to marry them. In Cockney English, you marry them what got you preggers. With this rapid remarriage, Grace felt a second loss, a betrayal of her Alicia by her love of a lifetime.

It could not have been easy for Grace to come and see that headstone with Alicia's birth and death on the right side and Steve's birth on the left side. Grace had tried to explain to Steve before he purchased the headstone that he was so young and that he might want to remarry at some point. The joint grave and preplanned headstone seemed to be too much of a commitment for a young man. Grace felt he was acting on the feelings of grief and was not allowing himself perspective. But he had assured Grace that he wanted to be buried with Alicia in that double plot. Now here he was, married again in less than six months.

Grace was sad about what had to feel like a betrayal of her daughter, but I saw in her behavior the pure love of Christ toward Steve. She had no resentment, guile, or judgment over what was happening. "I, the Lord, will forgive whom I will forgive, but of you is required to forgive all men."[51]. She even went to Steve's wedding. Woven in with her kindness and support for her deceased daughter's husband was a dose of reality. She told Steve she would always love him. She also told him that one day he would regret his precipitous behavior. And when he did, she would be there for him.

Grace was a welcome addition to my cemetery friends because I realized, yet again, that despite losing Claire, we were not handed Grace's problems. We had no son-in-law or his accompanying drama as part of the mix to cope with. We didn't have to make sense out of losing a child and then watch our child's spouse struggle.

But there was one more important lesson Grace offered. Her advice to me was the same she had given to Steve as she tried to talk him out of the rushed marriage, "Never make any major decisions in the first year after you lose a child." Alicia was not the first child Grace had lost, so she was seasoned. Seasoned, but not hardened. Tough, but still tender. Grace was someone to emulate for her strength and wisdom. I took Grace's advice and made no life-changing decisions in that first year. I count Grace's advice in the top ten pieces of advice I've been handed over a lifetime, one of which was, "Be sure to ask for an epidural during childbirth." Grace saved me from the pain of regrets. How fortuitous that a wise mother who had lost two children would become a part of my life at the cemetery? She was wise, caring, and bearing a burden greater than mine. She was my friend, a friend gained through an unnatural embrace.

24

THE WIND CHIMES

Claire has a pine tree just a few feet from her grave. Within a month after she was buried, I noticed that there was a set of wind chimes hanging from that pine tree. These were not your ordinary wind chimes. These wind chimes had a beautifully carved pink, white, and blue carousel horse at their center. Someone who knew Claire had hung the chimes.

When Claire was younger, she loved to go to a mall in our area that had a carousel. Perhaps it was the music. Maybe it was the motion, but she loved that carousel. I knew who the "someone" was. Claire's teacher, Jenn, had hung those chimes.

How did she find them? They were delicate in color and exquisite in detail, just like our Claire. It was as if they were made for Claire. The chimes would hang on the tree for one year—through rain, thunder, and dark of night. My other children and husband would touch the chimes as they went by the tree when they visited Claire's grave and say, "Hi, Claire!"

Sometimes a breeze would blow as I stood by Claire's grave and the chimes would ring. I fancied that Claire was breezing through, busy, just letting me know, as any now-twenty-year-old would, that she was going out again, wherever. The chimes were reassuring because of that feeling and the ease they gave to the men in my family when they made the visit to the cemetery. To me they were uplifting because someone else who knew Claire so well took the time to find this perfect gift and then bring it to the cemetery—and all anonymously. Claire's teacher, Jenn, had no expectation of thanks. But I called her and said, "It was you, wasn't it?" We shared a cry and then tromped down memory lane telling Claire stories. I am certain the wind chimes were in fast motion as we spoke.

As many times as I went to the cemetery alone, I realized from the teacher's gift that I was never really alone. Although they may not have called or visited, I began to recognize that those who knew Claire were also grieving, thinking of Claire, and coping. They really had not forgotten. I only wish I had a sort of existential sign-in book for those who were also coping with losing Claire so that I could thank them for the thoughts, prayers, and concern that I will never be able acknowledge. I understand that their strength was with me. I was looking for the worldly trappings of attention and physical presence. While searching for the prideful aspect of attention, I had lost sight of the inner strength that was growing with each visit.

25

FUNNY GUARDIAN ANGELS, AGAIN

W hen you lose a loved one, you soon realize that it will be some time before folks stop talking about her, and I don't mean friends and family. You will have medical bills and phone calls that will come almost daily during that first year. In our situation, doctor bills and lab bills were coupled with solicitations for Claire to join the Army. When the US military branches see someone over the age of 19 who is not attending school or working, they are all over them like flies on honey. Claire was a golden contact for military recruiters, and, because of the extent of her last illness, a prime target for questions about medical insurance and demands for payments from providers.

At first those phone calls and bills via US Postal Service are salt in the wound. What comes your way through claims folks and insurance statements is the experience of reliving the last illness of your loved one. Each time a recruiter calls or an "Uncle Sam Wants You" letter arrives, you dwell on dashed hopes. You find yourself during this period of settling up doing a significant amount of check-writing for the privilege of death's sting. When you are not writing checks, you are busy hounding insurers to ante up the dough for life's final medical bills. During this time, the customer satisfaction meter in me rose to the surface. The success rate of these medical care providers in providing services is irrelevant in their ability to collect payment from you. This concept of payment, despite great dissatisfaction with the result, is unique in the world of business. When was the last time you read about a company boasting of earnings from achieving the opposite of its goals and ignoring customer's desires? Yep, many of our customers are miserable because of our efforts and undesired results, but we still get paid.

I guess I can understand. A mechanic still gets paid for labor even when the conclusion he reaches is that your car cannot be repaired. But, the mechanic will feel almost as bad about his failure to find a repair as you do about the loss of a car and the beginning of the cash outlay for a new vehicle. Not so with insurers and the mechanics of medicine.

So many times during that first year, someone from a doctor's office or the medical insurance company would call and query, "Is Claire there?" Because our Claire was an adult in years, these folks presumed that they had to talk with Claire. The irony was that even when Claire was alive she never spoke a word because her disabilities were profound. It was difficult for me to say, "Claire died." I know people usually offer phrases with a finer point such as, "Claire passed," or "Claire passed away." However, I figured these medical mechanics should have been attuned, as it were, to the possibility of a loss, so I would hit them with blunt force. There are so many benefits with such brutal candor. The medical mechanics and insurers hardly know what to say. So, the phrase, "Claire's dead" seemed to be an icebreaker in terms of discussing whether some procedure was or was not covered under insurance. They are embarrassed, and any good negotiator will tell you, embarrassment in your worthy opponent gives you the advantage in terms of cost. Some providers and insurers can muster up some words of condolences, but most just want to get off the phone. Sometimes, all you get is, "Sorry," and a click. I have always enjoyed an awkward moment when I am the deliverer of such a moment and not the deliveree. In all that training we are told that we might be participating in once we get to a human in the punch-number systems of customer service ("Your call is being recorded and may be used for training purposes"), it is amazing to realize no one at any of these companies ever thought to pull up one of the "She's dead," calls in order to offer these poor automatons some training on death courtesy.

There was, however, one call that was surely the gift of a guardian angel. The voice on the other end of the phone sounded about twelve. I believe I could hear a little gum smacking from the other end of the phone. "Is Claire there?" I gave the usual, "Claire's dead." Training and perfunctory being what they are, sometimes the phone workers are not even listening or maybe my bombshell sounded like, "She's gone." This time I got something back and it was remarkable: "Do you know when she'll be back?"

"Yes," said I, "If the Book of Revelation has this correct, she should be here on the morning of the first Resurrection." The responses just got better as the smacking young girl offered: "I'll call back then." I shall put that appointment in my Day-Timer under the month of Millennium. I really hope they recorded that call and used it for training.

When I went to the cemetery that day, I smiled as I thought about some insurance claims person searching in vain for an appointment with Claire. There is humor in everything. Sometimes in our greatest moments of tension, the pressure valve is released when we realize that those we encounter may have been placed there to help. Jeffrey R. Holland once described their help as follows,

> I have spoken here of heavenly help, of angels dispatched to bless us in time of need. But when we speak of those who are instruments in the hand of God, we are reminded that not all angels are from the other side of the veil. Some of them we walk with and talk with—here, now, every day. Some of them reside in our own neighborhoods.[52]

I share Elder Holland's testimony of angels. I gained it through a year of acute notice of the help I received from those around me, however unwitting. God never does leave us alone or unaided in handling our challenges. The angels come and go, even when we don't realize it, but they are there. "I will go before your face. I will be on your right hand and on your left... my Spirit will be in your [heart], and mine angels around about you, to bear you up."[53] Sometimes, they just phone in to help.

26

THE PARENTS WHO DO NOT SPEAK OF THEIR LOSS

There were several sets of parents I bumped into (although not in the night, it being a cemetery and all and our aversion to things that go bump in the night) who were different from most. They never discussed their children, how they died, or their feelings. Big mistake. Their taciturn ways were a lesson as well. They were miserable.

Oh, they were pleasant souls when it came to speaking, but their misery emerged in an odd and obsessive way. Here are some snippets of conversations with the reticent parents.

"I don't like the grass they plant here. I filed a complaint and no one seems to do anything. I am going to plant some of my own."

They did and the result was this odd, clumpy grass that made their son's grave look uneven.

"We've had them dig up our son's headstone three times now, and it's still crooked. Well, just look at your daughter's headstone—it's uneven. Doesn't that make you crazy?"

I didn't have the heart to tell them I hadn't noticed it until they were kind enough to point it out! Still, the uneven, sinking headstone doesn't bother me. Quirky was our Claire, so why shouldn't she have these physical manifestations of that trait in her final resting place?

And one more...

"I called the mayor's office to complain about the sprinklers. There's not enough water here. I want more water—is that too much to ask?"

Rosencrantz and Guildenstern pointed out that among their team of caretakers they had about 150 years of caring for grass, shrubs, and all cemetery flora. Amateurish loved ones didn't understand the principles of horticulture and climate that they did, but the essentially unsatisfiable loved ones funneled all of their unexpressed grief into nagging the grave-diggers. They were missing something important, a lesson I had already learned, and one that would continue to be reinforced. You have to cope with the grief. You can't take it out on others or you become cranky, petty, and demanding. And if they were looking for the warmth of the Comforter, well, the Spirit does not dwell with the cranky and/or the petty and comes only upon heartfelt request, not demand. These cranky sorts were also missing out by harassing my gravediggers. They were losing a profound source of insight and solace.

If these grief-reticent parents were not dwelling on particulars or getting any results from their complaints to the locals, they would graduate to finding fault with the full cemetery complex. Over my 365-plus days, I heard everything from, "I don't really like this part of the cemetery," to "I wish we had purchased her plot in another cemetery," and all the way to, "I think we might have her exhumed."

I have never been convinced that it's a wise idea to be changing land-lords, leases, plots, and locations. That "rest in peace" thing ought to be taken seriously and carry some transfer constraints in it.

Demanding, obsessed with physical appearances of the graves, and not yet able to process their loss, these parents were a mess. They were unwilling to let their loss and grief do what it was supposed to do, and why death is indeed a part of life: it gets us to straighten out our priorities. Those who did not speak of their unspeakable loss turned their raw emotions into annoying negativity. Rosencrantz and Guildenstern told me that the cranks always complain, always criticize, and always find something else to fix no matter how hard they work to please them. One said, "We take all the verbal abuse because we know we're not the problem. They just haven't found their ways through the loss." Could these men be any wiser?

Grief is a raw emotion—it needs its relief valve. You can work it and all its pain through or you can vent at others on issues that are related only tangentially to what needs to be resolved. I understood exactly how the fault-finders felt because I nearly headed down the same path until my anthropological observations in the cemetery taught me who was recovering from their loss and who was not. My data set reached yet another unassailable conclusion: venting does not produce the healing—it begets more venting.

Losing someone so close to you forces painful introspection. Grief is a hard thing, and like Laman and Lemuel in the Book of Mormon, we want to murmur when "hard things" are asked of us by the Lord.[54] And the Lord does know all things and his eternal plan included these losses. But, Lehi counseled his murmuring and negative sons to just do the hard things. If we substitute murmuring for grief because of grief's pain, and you will end up like "grim" Miss Havisham—trying to hurt others who are innocent and certainly not responsible for your loss. Their Pip was the cemetery workers upon whom they seemed to be taking revenge because they happen to be employed at a cemetery. Their bitterness only added to their grief. Dickens had a sentence in *Great Expectations* that summed up what was happening to my picky-parent friends, "No varnish can hide the grain of the wood; and that the more varnish you put on, the more the grain will express itself."[55] Fix up and change the grave as much as you want, but you will not have worked through the loss that produced that grave. Venting is finding fault with others, an ultimately unsatisfying exercise that salts the wounds. Dickens described Miss Havisham and her life of devotion to unhealed grief: "…She had secluded herself from a thousand natural healing influences; that, her mind, brooding solitary, had grown diseased, as all minds do and must and will that reverse the appointed order of their Maker." 56

And what is the appointed order of our Maker? Well, part of His order is refining us through trials. The apostle Orson F. Whitney explained, "No pain that we suffer, no trial that we experience is wasted. It ministers to our education, to the development of such qualities as patience, faith, fortitude and humility. All that we suffer and all that we endure, especially when we endure it patiently, builds up our characters, purifies our hearts, expands our souls, and makes us more tender and charitable, more worthy to be called the children of God...and it is through sorrow and suffering, toil and tribulation, that we gain the education that we come here to acquire."[57] President Brigham Young summed it up by pointing to the fact that the trials are necessary for our salvation: "Every trial and experience you have passed through is necessary for your salvation."[58]

In an article that addressed fault-finding and its risks to our spiritual well-beings, Brother Mark Chamberlain wrote, "Perhaps part of the reason we all experience difficulties, weaknesses, and shortcomings in this life is so that we might have an opportunity to be more compassionate with others. We are truly all in this together. What a tragedy if we overlook our common humanness and point an accusing finger instead."[59] Rosencrantz and Guildenstern were there for them and with them, but the fault-finders missed common humanness as they focused on their flaws.

27

UNCLE ED, WORK FOR OUR KINDRED DEAD, SPIRIT PRISON, AND TWO LAWYERS

From the time I was old enough to have childhood memories until my high school years, I participated in my family's Memorial Day tradition. We all tumbled into as many cars as it took and spent Memorial Day traveling to cemeteries in and around Nanty-Glo, Pennsylvania. All the hot spots in western Pennsylvania that have coal mines and difficult pronunciations in common: Mundy's Corner, Ebensburg, Gallitzen—we toured them all. We had flowers for every grave, and my Uncle Ed brought along his grass clippers as well as gold paint to spruce up the medallions that rested on the graves of our relatives who were WWI and WWII veterans.

As a child you have a different perspective on Memorial Day because you are not old enough to appreciate that our country marks this day in order to honor those who gave the ultimate sacrifice. The depth of this holiday is lost on children. For a child, Memorial Day is the marking point for summer's start. School is done, and in the Eastern states, the pools, the parks, the ice cream joints, miniature golf courses, and beaches are open for business! The irony was that despite its open-of-the-season status, Memorial Day in western Pennsylvania was always cold and rainy—more like March than the beginning of summer. Nature foiled us despite our dreams of lazy, hazy days of summer. So, the day carried the pall of disappointment at its awful-weather dawn and went downhill from there with the cemetery car caravan. The cars were crowded, and we didn't have the luxury of seat belts in those pre–Ralph Nader "unsafe at any speed" autos. We were often sitting on top of each other and playing the usual childhood car game of who could rant the loudest, "She's touching me," or "She's looking at me." That game was accompanied by this game: who could ask the most times, "Is this the last cemetery?"

My father would calm us temporarily by promising us ice cream when we were done. Ice cream is all you need on a fifty-degree, rainy Pennsylvania day, but Memorial Day was the grand opening for all those notoriously local custard and ice cream stands. There were no Cold Stone Creameries open year-round and on every corner. Heck, Baskin-Robbins didn't even exist until I was in high school. Cold day, cold cemeteries, cold ice cream.

Each cemetery stop was agonizingly slow. My Uncle Ed moved at a glacial speed as he trimmed the grass around the headstones to his satisfaction. Then he painted. One drip of paint, even on the surrounding grass, and he cleaned. Then he brushed the grass trimmings. He was cautious, deliberate, and respectful. We, on the other hand, were whirling dervishes. "Respect for the dead!" my grandmother would mutter at us, and all to no avail. I did not know that I was in training.

I once begrudged my ancestors one day per year for a cemetery visit. When we lost our daughter, my 365-plus days at the cemetery found me muttering on Memorial Day to the glut of one-time visitors, "Novices!"

Over the course of my year of visits to Claire's grave, I acquired my own Uncle-Ed box of cemetery tools. My first purchase was a brush, actually an umpire's brush at the urging of my youngest son, John, who assured me that there was no brush as good for cleaning off debris and giving that smooth appearance. When summer came, the grass clippings overpowered the smaller umpire brush, so I bought a nice Ace ten-inch carpenter's brush. With summer came Phoenix monsoon and mud. I needed water for washing off the headstone, but Rozencrantz and Guildenstern turn off the water on weekends. I filled an empty Gain HE detergent bottle with water and carried it to the cemetery in my box, a plastic file box that was a left-over from tax season.

When the grass began to grow in the spring, I realized that Rosencrantz and Guildenstern mow weekly but edge monthly. The headstones get lost in the creeping grass. I bought myself a pair of clippers, a pair quite nearly identical to those my Uncle Ed used each Memorial Day.

As the summer wore on, carpal tunnel set in from the constant trimming of the grass around the edges of Claire's headstone. With an Ace Hardware coupon, I bought electric rechargeable clippers. They swoop along the edge, and they scalp so closely that you only need to power up the clippers about once each week. When my husband saw the Ace purchase, he stared, shook his head, and reflected that I might have gone round the bend on the cemetery thing.

Actually, the tools, box, and diligence were recompense for mocking my Uncle Ed. He took care of graves once each year, with great preparation and pride. I never understood nor appreciated his respect, his concern, and his love. My Uncle Ed maintained graves for those he had never known. He just understood they deserved gratitude expressed by service. This thought sounded familiar to me! I thought of our kindred dead and the need to serve them even when we have not known them in life. Work for the dead takes many forms, from cemetery to temple.

I am the only member of the Church in my family on this side of the veil. As a convert, the responsibility for my ancestors being given the opportunity to hear the gospel falls to me. I have worked on getting my ancestors' earthly ordinances completed since the time of my baptism. My husband and I have often taken our children to do baptisms for family names. We figure that with two lawyers leading the charge that day there is no way they are not getting out of spirit prison. However, it was my work at the cemetery that caused an exponential jump in both my efforts in and my success at temple work for my ancestors. In the year following Claire's death, the research on my family lines seemed inspired, and the names for temple ordinances flowed at such a pace that I had to enlist help from the ward because I could no longer do all the names in a timely manner without help from others. A brother in our ward told me, "Keep those name coming because you have been responsible for getting me to the temple each week." I wanted to correct him. Claire and Uncle Ed were responsible for getting him to the temple because of their inspiration at the cemetery. Uncle Ed's work had been completed years earlier, but the significance of his influence in my life was reemerging in my year at the cemetery.

My gardening/maintenance of Claire's grave paid tribute to another person—someone who understood the importance of work in dealing with a loss, my dear Uncle Ed. Idle hands are the devil's workshop. Well-maintained graves are a way of warding off idleness and maybe a few of the ghouls who seem to prefer messy and ill-maintained cemeteries.

What I learned in my maintenance tribute was that we often don't understand why others behave as they do until we have been through it. I have emerged from my year so completely different from the way I was when we first entered that cemetery. There's a good deal of humility. More important, there is the fully ingrained notion that we really are not in a position to judge until we have walked in the same shoes, or at least tried our hand at keeping the edges of a headstone trimmed neatly. For Uncle Ed—I wish I had been more of an apprentice rather than a whiner. Thank you for what I learned about cemetery maintenance under your tutelage. Thank you also for the symbolism your efforts were in reminding me about and reinvigorating our work for the dead. A mother's heart was turned to her departed daughter's resting place. The result was a literal manifestation of Malachi's promise that Elijah's restoration of the keys would "turn the heart of the fathers to the children, and the heart of the children to their fathers..." [60] We are one eternal round, Uncle Ed, Claire, and I.

28

CHILDREN AND THE CEMETERY

C hildren who lose a sibling are asked to deal with death in a way that most of their friends will never experience. When children lose a grandparent, aunt, or uncle, they are sad, but their daily lives do not change. They feel a void, but not a day-to-day change in how their house looks or its daily schedule. Further, a child's first experience with death is generally one that is a function of nature. Grandma was an octogenarian. Grandma has gone to be with Grandpa. They usually learn of death in life's natural order. But when a child loses a sister, his life changes completely. The presence of a child with significant disabilities and care requirements in a family means that everyone has assignments, all set up according to schedule. When Claire died, our children's daily schedule and chores changed completely. They were also dealing with the physical changes in our home: the empty bed, the clothes and shoes of their sister, hanging and sitting idly in her closet. They no longer had those daily assignments from Mom and Dad, "Go peek in on Claire and make sure she's sleeping," or "Go turn off Claire's feeding pump."

About a month after Claire's death, I heard my youngest son, John, tell a friend of mine that it was hard to walk by Claire's room and see an empty bed. But, he never really talked about Claire with me or my husband. I was afraid to bring up Claire's name because it seemed as if it was painful for him. Still, John was my most loyal companion to the cemetery. John would ring the chimes when we arrived at Claire's grave and again when we left. John would help me arrange the flowers for Claire's grave. He even learned to use the trimmer around the edges of the grave. He was a great helper, but so quiet when we visited and even more quiet on the ride home.

Sometimes we would stop by the cemetery as I was taking John and a friend to a movie or practice because it was on the way, and gas prices being what they were, well, the cemetery visit was combined with other errands. John would perform his usual task of chime-ringing and trimming. I noticed that John's friends would, however, stand back by the car. Few would come close to Claire's grave. I believe his young friends had the *NOTLD*/"Thriller" image of cemeteries in their minds.

On one visit, John's friend Mitchell walked right to the headstone with us. He stared at Claire's name and her date of death. He was quiet and respectful. He then looked over at John and said, "Sorry, John." For a thirteen-year-old boy with more braces than teeth, this tender moment was a landmark for John and me. John seemed to understand the tall order he had been handed because even at the most awkward of ages for teen boys, the two communicated. John was trying to understand the death of his older sister, a sister he had helped to care for and whom he loved. John seemed to understand that his life experience was different from those of all of his friends. And he seemed to understand that if his friend Mitchell felt sad that it had to be okay for him to feel sad about Claire.

I don't know any other way John would have experienced this sympathy and interaction unless we had been at the cemetery. The peaceful and gentle grandeur of the cemetery somehow touched Mitchell who then helped John with the harsh reality of not being able to see his sister until the next life. Claire's passing was etched in stone for John and Mitchell to see, and with a little help from a friend John had an epiphany. The Beatles had it right in the 60s, even if they were, as rumored, hallucinating. We do get by with that little help from our friends.

Perhaps the lesson here is for the friends of the grieving—you need not say much. All you have to do is be with them and offer a simple condolence.

We make things far more complicated than they need to be, and we begin to trot into territory that finds the grieving wondering if you really do want to help. "Sorry," is sometimes all we need.

Actor Jeff Conaway's untimely death as a result of an overdose occurred as I was finishing this manuscript. There were sad tributes to him and his ability. I was reading one that included a discussion about his most prominent role as Bobby Wheeler in the comedy series *Taxi*. In one episode he agreed to watch his friend Tony's two goldfish, George and Wanda. Not the most responsible person, Bobby neglected the fish while Tony was out of town. Tony returned to find George and Wanda deceased. Bobby knew that he had failed his friend, and he also was uncharacteristically acutely aware that he could not fix what had happened. Bobby still said just the right thing to his friend Tony, beautiful words, like young Mitchell's thoughts, in their simplicity, "I guess it was just their time." Sometimes there is no explanation anyone can offer, and attempts make it worse. "Sorry" is, however, perfect.

29

CHILDREN AND THE CEMETERY—PART 2

My older son, Sam, was a junior in high school when Claire died. He was also with us in Claire's room when she died. We would not have allowed him to be there if we had known she would go so quickly. Doctors had indicated weeks would go by, but our Heavenly Father knows better. As a result, Sam was just enjoying some time with Claire and happened to be there with us as Claire left this earth. He saw our panic, he saw our tears, he saw us trying to hold her, he saw the pulse oximeter dropping, and he saw her last breath. I was fifty-three years old before I saw someone die. He saw his sister die, and he was barely sixteen years old.

I worried about Sam because, like John, he did not talk about Claire or his being with her when she died. He seemed to pick up with his life as if nothing had happened. Sometimes it bothered me that he didn't show much emotion. He was also the most hesitant of any of our family to go to the cemetery. I could not get a sense of his struggles, but I knew something was just not right with him.

But, without my help, he found his way. He came home late from school one day and when I asked him where he had been he said, "I went to Claire's grave and spent some time. Everything is fine there." Then he went to his room and was quiet for hours.

The following week we were in the car together doing some errands, and I asked if he would mind if we stopped by Claire's grave. He said he would like to. When we arrived he stood back, away from the grave, and watched me do my Uncle Ed maintenance tasks. I resented his standoffishness. "This kid's callous," raced through my mind. Perturbed, I turned quickly to leave.

I realized as I was walking to the car that Sam was not with me. I turned around and saw him standing over Claire's grave. He wiped tears from his eyes. And then my six-foot-six teen kneeled down and gently patted Claire's headstone with his hand.

I spun around so quickly that my tears flew sideways. I also picked up my pace because I didn't think he wanted me to see the sensitive and healing moment he had just had.

When we got in the car, Sam finally spoke of Claire for the first time in six months, "Mom, it's not that I don't miss Claire. It's just that the cemetery is really hard for me."

I told Sam I understood, and as I said that to my dear son, I realized that we were just pulling out of the cemetery. The hallowed ground had once again done its magnificent work. We grieve in different ways. But we do heal.

Since that experience, Sam was called and completed a mission in Guatemala. He carries the last family picture we had with Claire, and I have counted six experiences he has described in his weekly e-mails where he was able to teach the gospel to an individual who had lost a loved one because he understood their pain. But, he also understood that the cemetery is not where our dear Claire is—she lives. She lives because of the atonement. Sam's testimony of that atonement was tried, tested, and reemerged, a gift that has allowed him to teach the gospel.

I suspect that Claire has been with him on his mission, overseeing his work and the doors that have been opened because Sam understands what it is like to lose someone you love so much at such a young age. The two of them have been a dynamic missionary team.

I recall reading President Ronald Rasband's April 2010 priesthood session talk on calling missionaries, in which he described sitting with President Henry Eyring as he issued missionary callings: "I remember Elder Eyring using very sincere words, asking the Lord to bless him to know 'perfectly' where the missionaries should be assigned."[61] The story of President Rasband's experience of sitting with Elder Eyring as he issued missionary calls is touching and reaffirming of my belief that Sam was sent where he needed to be:

A couple of other times as the process moved along, Elder Eyring would turn to me and say, "Well, Brother Rasband, where do you feel this missionary should go?" I would name a particular mission and Elder Eyring would look at me thoughtfully and say, "No, that's not it. He would continue to assign the missionaries where he had felt prompted. As we were nearing the completion of that assignment meeting, a cipture of a certain missionary appeared on the screen. I had the strongest prompting, the strongest of the morning, that the missionary we had before us was to be assigned to Japan. I did not know that Elder Eyring was going to ask me on this one, but amazingly he did. I rather tentatively and humbly said to him, "Japan?" Elder Eyring responded immediately, "Yes, let's go there. And up on the computer screen the missions of Japan appeared. I instantly know that the missionary was to go to the Japan Sapporo Mission.

Elder Eyring did not ask me the exact name of the mission, but he did assign that missionary to the Japan Sapporo Mission.[62]

Guatemala is a harsh country with too many young widows and widowers and where heartless conditions take young children from this life too soon. Sam's calling there was, as President Eyring seeks to do, a "perfect" one because he had experienced up front, close, and personally, the kind of loss that left the dear and good people there struggling to understand. Sam's struggle with the loss of his sister prepared him to serve in a way that touched so many hearts and softened them for receiving the gospel. During his mission he has seen a young father shot and killed, and another young man taken during what was not a dangerous surgery for removal of a tumor on his leg. These are inexplicable and painful losses to their families, but our Sam is there with the compassion, empathy, insight, and "Preach My Gospel" at the ready.

"There's always a reason," and "When the Lord closes a door, he opens a window." I heard those phrases time and again during my 365-plus days of cemetery visits. At first the phrases seemed condescending and trite. However, phrases last this long in our folklore because we find through our individual experiences that they are true. Claire's earthly life ended, but she has gone on to bless our lives along with the lives of others who seek truth in the face of loss. Sam opened doors and windows on his mission because of his deep understanding of earthly life's temporary nature and the power of eternal salvation. I will spend an eternity understanding the other reasons for her life and death and finding the windows she opened.

30

BRENDA

Brenda is Alex's grandmother. I met Brenda and another grandmother one afternoon at the cemetery on a stop that I had made as I headed home from work. The conversation began like so many others among and between women—they liked my suit. When I learned that Brenda was Alex's grandmother, I shared with her that I had met her son early on in my 365-plus days of visits and that his taking the initiative to speak to me had made a big difference in my recovery. The three of us commiserated that day about how people tend to forget that the wound is still fresh for months. We also noted how much we hated the lectures about moving on with our lives. We reached unanimous consent, "We are stubborn, and we were not ready."

Brenda gave me her e-mail address and said she had a little help with a daily e-mail called "365 days of grieving." You sign up for it (through Google you can find it through most funeral homes by typing in "365 days of grieving"), it's free, and each morning there was a thought from someone who had lost a loved one accompanied by a scripture and a little prayer. I will owe Brenda forever for giving me that gift. She had solved the problem of "No one cares anymore," because there, each day, was a message for me. I had mail! Better yet—I had coping-with-grief e-mail. When I read the stories of others and their grief journeys, I felt reassured that this too shall pass.

For me, at the point I received my Brenda gift, grief groups were awkward. I had progressed more than most who attend grief sessions. I stopped speaking of Claire to my friends because even those closest to you grow weary. You want them to know you are progressing. If you are progressing a little too slowly, then they feel that they are Bill Murray in *Groundhog Day*. They are on a different day now and expect the same from you. Counselors carry that inherent conflict of interest that stems from revenue-flow need. What I needed to know was whether I was, as many people said, "getting weird." These daily e-mails were free, private, insightful, real, and reassuring. What truly made a difference for me was that each message had a scripture from the Bible. I read my grief e-mail the first thing each morning and found the same feelings that I had seen at the cemetery—there were people who had it worse. Grief is not easy for anyone. But, these messages demanded faith because they were using scripture to pull us along.

I realized from my daily dose of coping e-mail that I was not the first to trod grief's complex maze. I didn't invent the feelings, and I didn't have to reinvent the wheel to find ways to cope. I had the answer—rely on scriptures. My scripture reading became more diligent, more inquisitive, and more searching. I was looking for answers, and they are there if we just have the patience to keep at the hard work of pondering what we read. Doctrine and Covenants Section 121 can see you through anything. It was given to the Prophet Joseph Smith as he was unjustly held prisoner, knowing that he would die a martyr. The prophet pleads with the Lord, wondering how long He will allow the injustices to continue. The Lord responds in verses 7 and 8: "My son, peace be unto thy soul; thine adversity and thine afflictions shall be but for a small moment; And then, if thou endure it well, God shall exalt thee on high." But, there is much more in Section 122—the Lord's reminder, in the words of Jiminy Cricket to Pinocchio, "to buck up": "The Son of Man hath descended below them all. Art thou greater than he?"[63] The Lord has experienced whatever we are feeling and knows what we need.

Job was lectured by the Lord for not understanding that we don't understand how the laws of nature operate: "Hast thou given the horse strength? hast thou clothed his neck with thunder? Canst thou make him afraid as a grasshopper? he mocketh at fear, and is not affrighted;"[64] The Lord is in charge, and He does know everything, including what we can and cannot do. He knows that we can make it through grief's darkest moments and deepest challenges.

Turn to any conference and reread the talks given by our general authorities. You cannot find a conference where those who love and lead us have not advised, "Read your scriptures, say your prayers, attend your meetings, do your calling, and get to the temple." During my 365-plus days at the cemetery, I remember thinking in response to this wisdom, "Yes, but I have real problems here. I need a little something more." Pride had interfered with my ability to trust that their counsel could see me through grief's challenges. Brenda brought me back around to the scriptures—back to the basics. I took an indirect route through the cemetery and a nonmember's advice, but I made my way back to the counsel that does indeed work.

I find myself giving out the daily grief e-mails to others because it is a powerful tool for reorientation—back to scriptures. I sent the grief e-mail site along to a friend who lost her mother after caring for her for three years. She sent me a note with the following, "I love this. I get an e-mail each morning that seems to say someone understands. I have also picked up the Bible, something I haven't done in years." Indirect, but she got to where she needs to be.

31

THE BIKE RIDES

Terry and I had not done much together during Claire's life. Because of her disabilities, one of us was always home with her. We did not have the mom-and-dad nights out, even at a minimal level. If all was well, we would make it out for our anniversary. So rare was our time outside our home together that when Claire died, it was traumatic for us to ride together in the same car. Being together in the car was a brutal reminder of our loss. We were just awkward in our time together—like two people on a blind date. When Claire died, we had been married for thirty years. And after thirty years of marriage with the missing link of Claire, we were not at all sure how to act together outside our home. We knew how to care for Claire together. We knew how to schedule our lives so that someone was always home with Claire. But, we didn't know how to be with each other in a setting other than home. We had to find our relationship.

The cemetery was the means for our adjustment. Each Saturday, at least until Phoenix reached its one hundred and ten degrees, we rode the seven miles to the cemetery and seven miles back. We rode, we talked, and then we visited Claire's grave. Here was a logical transition of still having our Claire as a focus but getting used to the idea that it was now okay to spend time together.

While we were at the cemetery on our weekly visits, Terry had the chance to meet some of my cemetery friends. When we were riding to and from and the cemetery, we had the chance to reflect on her life. When we stopped at a Water 'n Ice store for a drink, we had the chance to sit together in something as close to a restaurant that we had experienced in over twenty years. When you have a special needs child, you have the experience of rendering daily and much-needed service. You can feel the definition of Christlike charity as you fulfill the role of someone who serves a role that no one else can. But, parents who fill this role with a child don't go out to dinner together. The most we ever spent in a year at restaurants while Claire was alive was ninety-five dollars! We had to rotate going to baseball games, ward functions, and even wedding receptions. Friends, neighbors, and ward members joked that we must really just be one person because no one ever saw us together. So, after twenty years of the fire drills of rotating caring for Claire, we had to learn to be together again, to function as a couple.

After a few months of cemetery bicycle jaunts, we realized what Claire was doing for us, even from beyond the veil. Our connection to Claire was the key to becoming a couple again. The peacefulness of the cemetery was a draw for us, a magnet that drew us to each other once again. Sometimes as we stood together over her uneven headstone that one of the cranks had so kindly observed, we could feel Claire. I believe she was looking down at us and saying, "I'm fine, and, by the way, you two look great together."

32

BRENDA AND BILL

Sometimes when we rode to the cemetery, Terry and I would run into Brenda and her husband, Bill. In fact, Brenda and Bill walked the perimeter of the cemetery several times every morning for almost six months. They had been so close to their grandson that the cemetery was also helping them with their adjustment. Despite the loss of their first grandchild in such a tragic way, Brenda and Bill were upbeat and happy. I never saw them not smiling. The pain was there, but so was their determination to get through it. They had to develop the strength to help their daughter.

Their faith was strong, indeed; it was compelling. Brenda had an interesting way of reflecting. She would sometimes describe the last days of Alex's short life, but then she would talk about the blessings in her life and always finish with, "God is good."

Just a few months after Alex's funeral, Bill was hit by a careless driver and his car was totaled. He was injured, but not seriously. Here was a family that had lost a grandchild and was trying to cope with the void when they were hit, literally and figuratively, with another astronomical odds incident. After they told us the story of the accident, Brenda added, "God is good." Bill was alive, the insurance company will replace the car—all fixable.

As eerie as it was, Brenda used the experience of the accident to reflect on the two kinds of problems I had discovered in my course of recovery: fixable and unfixable. Brenda had reached the same conclusion that had come to me in reflecting on our loss of Claire: The fixable ones, she said, you just fix. Brenda said that with the loss of your first grandchild, well, you have an unfixable problem and you walk and work it through and remain grateful for all the other blessings in your life. In her cemetery time and contemplation, Brenda had discovered the very same insight that had come to me. We are taught that if we have questions, we should study, ponder, and pray. Indeed, this restoration is based on a young boy following that formula: "If any of you lack wisdom, let him ask of God, that giveth to all men liberally, and upbraideth not; and it shall be given to him."[65] In this process of grieving, what we both needed was wisdom and insight. All we had to do was ask. Our quiet times at the cemetery were giving us the time for reflection so that the answers could come through to the questions we had about life and death. Brenda's similar conclusions helped me to understand that not only do the answers come to those who seek, but the answers are identical, particularly when it comes to grappling with the "Whys" that accompany grief.

I began to see the world through Brenda's "God is good" glasses. I still had three terrific kids who were sensitive and mature and who had life's adventures ahead of them. I had no debts. I had a father who called me every day to make sure I was okay. I had one of my sisters who would send me a card nearly once each week to offer a thought, some humor, and to let me know she was thinking of me. My other two sisters called to see how I was coping. God was indeed good. My cemetery friend Brenda and I had been given wisdom.

33

YOU'RE GONNA
NEED A BIGGER BOAT:
A LIFE OF PREPARATION

There was one additional lesson that Brenda taught me about coping with grief. She had lived the type of life that had prepared her for coping. In our snippets of conversations, I learned that Brenda and Bill had moved Brenda's mother out to live with them so that they could care for her. I also learned that Brenda was a volunteer for several organizations, including one that helped young women through their single-mom pregnancies and offered counsel and resources on adoption. Brenda had lived a rich life that focused on helping others. Bill had his share of health problems and she cared for him, in everything from the daily walks to a heart-smart diet.

Before she lost her grandson in such an unjust and painful way, Brenda was already a person of great depth, and when her loss came she had that deep pool to draw from. I suspect that the pioneers who lost children as they crossed the plain were also members of great depth for we know from church history how diligently they served, how much they had given for the building of the kingdom, and how willing they were to leave everything behind for the opportunity of living their faith free of fear and hostility.

Brenda taught me of the importance of preparation for the challenges and trials we cannot know or anticipate. When he was president, John Kennedy offered this thought during his first year in office: "The time to repair the roof is when the sun is shining[66] Our stake president, Reece Bawden, frequently reminds us that sometimes the Lord calms the treacherous seas we are in and sometimes he calms the sailor, steadying the hand of those who must weather the storm. But I add one more possibility from what I gained from observing Brenda. We are like Chief Brody (Roy Scheider) in the movie *Jaws*, after he sees the great white shark for the first time. He turns to Captain Quint (Robert Shaw) and offers that third possibility, "You're gonna need a bigger boat." I was trying to deal with a twenty-three-foot great white, and my spiritual preparation was more along the lines of dealing with a sand shark. The parable of the ten virgins teaches us this.[67] The five prepared bridesmaids were not selfish; you can't transfer spiritual readiness. You have to build it, grow it, and keep at it, never knowing when you are going to need it. No one can transfer spiritual depth when you need it—it has to be there or you have to grow it.

Brenda's life had been a Christlike life. And although she felt the acute pain of losing her first grandchild, she was able to cope and adjust better than I because of all that she had done to that point. Grief goes down easier when we have developed the spiritual depth that comes from study, reflection, and selfless service to others.

34

THE CLEAN SWEEP PART 2: TRINKETS AND LEGACIES

Claire's wind chimes had hung on the tree by her grave for almost a year. When my beloved Rosencrantz and Guildenstern had done the first clean sweep in July, they had left her discreet chimes in the tree. When the second sweep came, just shy of the one-year mark of Claire's death, I did not worry about taking the chimes down because I fancied that they were immune from the sweep. But, on the day following the clean sweep, I arrived to find that the chimes were gone. I was devastated. The kids and I had rung those chimes each time we visited. Their sound signaled that we had arrived at Claire's place. "Hi, Claire," was our mantra as we made the chimes sing. Now they had been taken in one fell swoop with the sweep.

I went to the office and the librarian-voiced woman told me that they did keep the clean-sweep articles in a pile in the back of the office building for a few days. I had tears. The librarian-voiced woman called for Rick, the supervisor, to come help. The head of Rosencrantz and Guildenstern,

Inc. got the cemetery golf cart used for "carting" people around for picking gravesites, and he drove me around to the clean-sweep pile to help me find Claire's chimes. He took one pile, I took another, and together we searched. Within fifteen seconds, Claire's merry-go-round chimes came to the surface, fully intact. I smiled at Rick even as I cried, "What are the chances?" I asked. "Really slim," he said, and he was as happy as I was.

I also had an odd feeling of melancholy because I stood and looked for a moment at the clean-sweep pile. Here were the treasures loved ones had put on graves. I felt as if I were invading their privacy. I could see a bottle of Tabu cologne. There was a can of Sprite. There were items of jewelry. There were so many photos—some of individuals, some of couples, and some of teens on their prom night. There were decks of cards, cans of Coors, and packs of Twinkies. I even noticed one Monopoly game piece—the top hat. There were Mardi Gras beads and lots of toy cars, some of them Corvettes and Mercedes, choices that I gather symbolized actual ownership or dreams of those who now lived in a world that has no need of combustion engines, let alone German-built or fast ones.

I read in the *New York Times* that Barbara Stuart who played Miss Bunny, Sgt. Carter's girlfriend from the *Gomer Pyle* television series, died on May 15, 2011. The highlighted quote in the article read, "A familiar face who found steady work, but not quite stardom, over five decades."[68] I read the *New York Times* each day just to aggravate myself, and this quote gave me my aggravation quota for the day. She had led a full life with her husband and stepchildren and was content to retire quietly in the non-star-occupied beauty of St. George. She was content to have been a memorable character—diva was not her style. The measurement of our lives looks different from the perspective of loss. Every man's death diminishes us because of who they are spiritually, not by worldly rank or possession.[69]

Standing among the clean-sweep treasures brought another epiphany. Ashes to ashes and dust to dust.[70] No matter how important material things were to us in this life, they end up in the clean-sweep pile for a nice trip to the dump. These trinkets are symbols of a life, but they are not the meaning of life. When I leave this life, I don't want the Tabu cologne bottle on my headstone; I want my children to remember the smell of my cologne when I held them close. I don't want them to put the Monopoly game piece on my headstone—I want them to remember the times I soaked them for the cash when they landed on Boardwalk. I want them to know that I was happy driving whatever car I owned, so long as it was reliable.

And when we have finished our work here on the earth, what happens to our stuff? Clean-sweep pile. I think of the sacrifices of the women in the early days of the Church who surrendered their china so that the walls of the Kirtland Temple could have a beauty worthy of the building's purpose. As a new member of the Church with my only assets being my student loans, I marveled at their ability to surrender so precious a material good. After my experiences with the clean sweeps at the cemetery I realize that these women left a legacy that would not have been possible if they had kept their dishes.

Standing among the clean-sweep trinkets taught me to take care with my legacy. The vivid memories have to be created. The trinkets of symbolism are just that: trinkets. The stories that go with them have captured my imagination each day in the cemetery. I have learned to answer this question in my choices and actions: "How will they remember me?" The trinkets are irrelevant—it's how you used them that matters.

35

RICK

There is more to the story about Rick and the clean-sweep pile. I thanked him for helping me, and I turned to walk back to my car. He refused to allow that and offered me a ride in the cart. As we rode along that cool January day, I thanked him for the cemetery. I explained how much coming here over the past year had helped me and that I appreciated the care that he and his staff took to make it a peaceful park. Rick began to speak with a great sense of pride about what his work does for people.

He said that his job involved so much more than caring for the grounds. He said that he loved his job because he felt that he had really helped people over the years. Rick told me that he once saw a woman at her mother's grave every day over a period of months. Rick assured me that she did not approach my record, but he worried because each day she cried at her mother's grave. Eventually he stopped to talk with her. She had cared for her mother for years, and after her mother died she felt lost. Those who care for the terminally or chronically ill all feel an acute void when their patient leaves them. It isn't just that they are gone. As a caregiver, you have been forced to find a new and different purpose and set of activities in life.

On the day that Rick stopped to talk, the woman told Rick that she was so distraught that she wanted to take her own life. Rick said that he assured her that things would get better. He made it a point after that experience to talk with her each day when she visited her mother's grave. As Rick explained it, his years of experience at the cemetery have taught him about grief and how to help those who are struggling with it. As Rick phrased it, "We just hashed through a lot of feelings." Then, one day, Rick noticed she did not come and he worried. He said he even found himself checking the papers to see if something had happened. It would be a week before she returned, but when she did, she sought out Rick and thanked him. She had found a new job and finally felt ready to move on. Rick said he only responded with, "I told you things would get better." Rick felt he had made some small difference in someone's life.

I then found myself asking Rick for advice. Who would know better about long-term grief? I explained that I was now passing the one-year mark and was getting worried about my coming each day. He was so calm when he responded, "I've been here a lot of years. I see a lot of grief. I watch as people work it through. Here's what I've learned—you will know when it's time to move one. Oh, you'll still visit, but you won't feel the need to come here every day. It's a different amount of time for everyone. But they all find their way."

I got out of the golf cart, thanked Rick, and felt great. From the mouth of an expert, I had reassurance and advice. Rick, not a Mormon, understood the principle of Doctrine and Covenants 58:4, "For after much tribulation come the blessings." I had the blessing of Rick and the hope of moving along after my 365-plus visits to the cemetery. How lucky it was that the chimes went into the clean sweep. How fortunate that Rick, a city employee, happened to be yet another angel sent to help.

36

THE CRITTERS: UNAUTHORIZED

There are only two species of critters in a cemetery: authorized and unauthorized. Unauthorized include dogs. Signs at both entrances of the cemetery state very clearly, "No Dogs Allowed." Dogs are unauthorized. So are cats, but who can control cats? The saying "herding cats" does have its foundation in fact.

Despite the warnings about unauthorized critters (canines), you would be stunned at the number of people who bring their dogs to the cemetery. Worse, as they visit, they allow their dogs to gallop about (and some of them are large enough to work up a stampede gallop), relieving themselves on graves and headstones alike.

What are they thinking? Like my grandmother shouting as we hooligans leaped and cavorted around the cemeteries on Memorial Day, I found myself waving my arms and restraining a shout of, "Respect for the dead!" The unauthorized dogs in the cemetery were part of a larger societal issue that dismisses propriety. There are certain things you just don't do, no matter how casual we become. Dogs in the cemetery would be one of them.

I began a quest. Each time I saw a dog in the cemetery, I spoke to its owner, "I don't know if you were aware, but dogs are not allowed in the cemetery. There is a reason for this rule. It's out of respect for the dead." My words were carefully chosen and meant to be an explanation.

The amazing thing about my self-designated cemetery dog sheriff role was the universal and respectful response, "I'm so sorry. I didn't know." No anger. No dog rage. No arguing. Perhaps it's the spiritual quality of the cemetery. Perhaps it is just an ability to receive a polite education on graveyard etiquette, or perhaps they can sense that I am worried about the amazing quality of this non-*NOTLD* cemetery. All the dog owners have been receptive, and, subsequently, reformed.

I learned it doesn't hurt to speak up when you have a legitimate concern. I learned that people have a heightened respect for hallowed ground. I learned that we still are willing to hold to absolutes. I learned that people can be corrected gently for the sake of a better world. How I wish life outside the cemetery would allow propriety and gentle correction to play its necessary role.

But, I learned one more thing—the manner of correction may be the key to respectful responses. I really did want to say, "Are you out of your mind? What kind of person brings a dog to the cemetery?" However, the soft answer does turn away wrath.[71] And when we are "reproving betimes," the follow-up of love is important.[72] When I saw my "dog friends" after my gentle persuasion encounters, I always inquired about them and how they were weathering their storms of grief. When we avoid these difficult conversations, we may miss the opportunity of friendship. Difficult conversations need love at the foundation. In a society that videotapes difficult conversations for reality shows that find audiences cheering one person's humiliation, we are teetering on the loss of graciousness. Reproving betimes with love is a lost art, but not in the cemetery.

37

THE CRITTERS: AUTHORIZED

The authorized critters in the cemetery are the birds, the snails, the butterflies, and bees. I feel sorry for the cemetery bees. You see them diving into huge sunflowers, surely thinking that a feast awaits, and then their noses (or whatever bees have) are bopped. You swear you can almost see them dazed, flying away in a drunk's circular and slower pattern. It's rare when there are real flowers on the headstones. Apart from the day of the funeral and an occasional live rose brought to rest on the headstone, folks opt for artificial flowers. They keep longer, look better, and can be arranged with those internal wires providing more flexibility. Live flowers among the dead seems wrong. It's just that the bees can't tell the difference. Michael's has done a fine job in its floral offerings. Michael's has fooled Mother Nature, or at least her bees.

The birds also are fooled by the flowers. When folks place the large sunflowers on the grave, you can see where the birds have aimed for the center of the sunflowers, gotten a beak full of plastic and fuzz, and spit it out on the ground near the grave. Poor birds.

But the birds' frustrations were a lesson for me. Nothing alive here—these are memorials. We can visit and we can look, but our loved ones have moved on to a new life in a more gracious place. And so we too need to move on. I learned from the flora and the fauna.

38

THE GRAVEYARD AT NIGHT

Although Claire's final resting place was not a *NOTLD*/"Thriller" cemetery, coming to a cemetery at dusk seemed to be pushing my luck just a tad. Whistling past a graveyard is one thing. Traipsing about a cemetery when it is dark, well, it seemed to be demanding a bit much of any potential ghouls to tolerate our presence there if they have it reserved for night use.

So, it would be eight months, and quite by accident, that I found myself at the cemetery as darkness fell. I was late coming home from work and thought the gates might be closed, but despite darkness, they were wide open. I drove in, admittedly with trepidation.

I noticed the large number of solar lights relatives had placed on graves. There is something ironic about our thinking that spirit-like deceased relatives need a night-light. They have gone on to live in light and truth. But, when those solar lights are on the graves in the baby section, your heartstrings feel a little tug. No matter what your religious conviction or your beliefs about the certainty of the hereafter, there is something to be said for leaving the night-light on for a toddler.

There is an overabundance of night-lights in the baby section. As it should be. Perhaps this act of normalcy, of performing the mundane parental task of leaving the night-light on, gives the parents some role in the life of their small child. Why do they need a night-light? They don't, but their parents need the comfort of that small act of service for a child they can no longer kiss good night. In the words of the great John Lennon, "Whatever gets you through the night."[73] He meant that for the parents. The history of the song is actually grounded in religion. Mr. Lennon was watching television in the wee hours and stopped to listen to a sermon Reverend Ike, a televangelist, was giving. The purpose of the sermon was to encourage those who are in despair to use their faith. Mr. Lennon copied down this sentence from the sermon: "Let me tell you guys. It doesn't matter. It's whatever gets you through the night."[74] Their children are fine, but as parents, they still need a role and a solar light goes a long way in fulfilling that need, or maybe providing some answers for what we seek.

Light is what we, those who remain behind, seek. Perhaps we seek it because we know our loved ones are basking in that light. Whether it be truth, insight, understanding, or something to help us along this life's paths, light is the answer. In the beginning of the world and scripture, there is, "Let there be light."[75] In every standard work, we find light, literally and figuratively: "...I will be a light unto them forever, that hear my words."[76] Our Savior said, "I am the light of the world."[77] At the time of His birth, there was no darkness—even at night![78] At the time of His death until His Resurrection, there was no light; not even a match could be struck.[79] "That which is of God is light; and he that receiveth light, *and continueth in God,* receiveth more light; and that light groweth brighter and brighter until the perfect day."[80] And His light that leads us is "kindly":

Lead kindly Light, amid th' encircling gloom;
Lead thou me on!
The night is dark, and I am far from home;
Lead thou me on![81]

We follow the light. We need the light. We seek the light, and we even do it symbolically at the cemetery. A solar shepherd's hook light is a form of a testimony in cemeteries. Those who place them there understand their healing power—they seek the light because they know its comfort and promise for them and their loved one who has gone on the next, completely light, stage of eternal progression.

39

HE WON'T BE HERE FOR LUNCH ANYMORE

I used to see him in the southeast corner of the cemetery section where Claire's grave is located. He was there each day, around lunchtime, in his green-and-white folding chair. He usually wore a white jacket. Most days he had on a hat. His legs were always crossed, and he seemed calm, as if he were on a beach just taking in the ocean breezes. He brought along his lunch and enjoyed it at his leisure as he sat quietly. He was a fixture. He was too far away to speak and, at that point, I was too early in my healing process to work up the nerve to take the walk over to speak with him.

One day I noticed that he, his chair, and his lunch were not there. Then I noticed that he missed several days consecutively. The days continued to click by and there was still no sign. My friend in the green-and-white lawn chair would not return. Rick told me that this loyal lunch visitor was fairly typical. "Men who lose their wives don't do as well as when husbands go first. You see it all the time. They come here and sit by their wives' graves. Then it is only a matter of a few months before we are preparing for their funerals."

Ah, the gravediggers and their wealth of information and skills of observation, nay even epidemiological studies. "They want to be with their wives, and they've lived good long lives." Rick is so wise and observant. The natural order of things goes on, and perhaps these widowers no longer fight to hang on to this life. Their beloveds have moved on, and being with their sweethearts is what they want, not the void and loneliness. Somehow, nature steps in and expedites her work. More likely Providence grants them their wish of a reunion.

Rick did not see these octogenarian husband-and-wife stories as sad ones, tragic loss upon tragic loss for their children and grandchildren. Rather, Rick saw these stories as the culmination of love stories. "They should be together," was his thought.

More than his wisdom and observations, I appreciated Rick's calmness. Here's a man who has truly made peace with the end of this portion of life's journey. He has no worries or fears about those he meets or those he buries for he has seen true love. He has witnessed the romantic notion of husband's lunch each day at his wife's graveside. Love marches on. On occasion, the lovers are temporarily separated, but they do find their ways back to each other. Our job is to recognize the joy they feel even as we grapple with their departure from us. "That's so sad," was my initial reaction when Rick told me of our friend's passing in order to explain his absence at lunchtime. But Rick offered his certainty about life after death, "He's fine. He's with his sweetheart now every day, and not just for lunch."

As Rick spoke I understood the testimony I had gained of our eternal existence and the unassailable truth that we will be with our loved ones. I hadn't had my sweet Claire come to me in a vision and affirm that she was okay. I heard no voices. I only had the strength of a testimony gained at the cemetery with a little help from friends and angels alike. Elder Dallin H. Oaks of the Quorum of the Twelve taught: "Visions do happen. Voices are heard from beyond the veil. I know this. But these experiences are exceptional…Most of the revelation that comes to leaders and members of the Church comes by the still, small voice or by a feeling rather than by a vision or a voice that speaks specific words we can hear. I testify to the reality of that kind of revelation, which I have come to know as a familiar, even daily, experience to guide me in the work of the Lord."[82] It seemed odd to me that a man and a green lawn chair would mean so much to me in understanding eternity, but I had to admit that if you are listening for the "still, small voice," a green lawn chair seems like a logical prop for the arrival.

40

BECAUSE THEY ARE HERE, I AM ALIVE

In the older part of the cemetery, I noted five graves, one after the other, with similar headstones. I also noticed that the graves were kept up immaculately and that there were always large bunches of skillfully arranged silk flowers in each vase of each of the five headstones on each of the five graves. The five graves were those of five children, all of whom had died when they were young. All I could think of when I first saw those five graves, all children of the same parents, was, "How does a parent cope with the loss of five children?"

I knew from the dates of death for each of the children that the parents of these children could no longer be alive, unless people in Mesa, Arizona, lived to the ripe old age of 130 to 150 years. Old Testament times saw some fairly long-in-the-tooth souls, but pioneer Mesa found its residents receiving Father Time's call in their seventies or earlier. So, the mystery became, "Who maintains these five graves so beautifully?"

I was at the cemetery each day, and always at different times, but I never seemed to see anyone at the five graves. Still, I would know someone had been there because the flowers were changed as they started to become worn and faded. Who was the mysterious caretaker?

Finally Rosencrantz and Guildenstern, my gravediggers who take it all in at the cemetery, explained. There was a sixth child born, and he was the caretaker for the graves. He told Rozencrantz and Guildenstern once that he would always be grateful for the lives of these five brothers and sisters, "Because of them I am alive."

I didn't quite follow the connection or the logic, but my gravediggers explained that because the couple kept losing children, they kept trying again and again to have more children. It was not until the sixth child (who would become the caretaker) that they beat death's grip on their family. The caretaker of the graves, Child Number 6, felt that if any of the children had survived, his mother would have stopped having children. Lucky Number 6 wanted his siblings to know how grateful he was and how much he cared—to do the very best for the brothers and sisters he would not meet until the next life.

John Donne's thoughts came to mind. "No man is an island, entire of itself; every man is a piece of the continent, a part of the main. If a clod be washed away by the sea, Europe is the less, as well as if a promontory were, as well as if a manor of thy friend's or of thine own were: any man's death diminishes me, because I am involved in mankind, and therefore never send to know for whom the bells tolls; it tolls for thee."[83]

The indomitable human spirit lives in the cemetery. Like Job, these parents of the five took loss after loss and kept trying, willing to risk the pain for the joy of bringing one life into this world. And what a child he was, someone who recognized his role in the birth order and spent a lifetime honoring others for their short mortal lives. I have often imagined that when this caretaker sixth son moves along to the next life that the five siblings who greet him will know him well. How could they not after all the care he had given to them? There are ties that bind across the veil when we take the time to serve them.

41

MADD

You never meet the family of a drunk driver in the cemetery. But throw a rock in any direction in a cemetery and you can find the headstone of an innocent victim killed by a drunk driver. I have met the families of the innocent victims killed by drunk drivers. My father used to say that drunks always survive their accidents because their bodies are loosey-goosey and they bounce freely during an accident; nothing breaks. Sober folks know what's coming and, justifiably, are scared and rigid and, as a result, become, as a Bronxite would say, "the stiffs."

There is no easier way to say this, so not to put too fine a point on things: Drunks kill. The deaths they cause are worse than any of the other causes of death in the cemetery because they are unexpected and senseless. Some deaths, such as car accidents, are unexpected. But, we at least know that accidents do happen. Some deaths are senseless: the suicides and the drug overdoses. But the deaths at the hand of drunk drivers are both unexpected and senseless, and that combination has an exponential effect on grief and puts the skids on the healing process. I have met the wife and mother of a forty-two-year-old father killed when a drunk driver turned in front of him. The drunk is alive and well and in prison. The wife, mother, and children carry the strain of their sudden loss on their faces. When you hug them, they sob and ask aloud in the same monosyllabic way, "Why?"

Of all the losses in the cemetery, the loss of life to a drunk driver is one I still cannot explain. Of all the relatives and friends I have met in this cemetery, those whose loved ones' lives have been taken by drunk drivers suffer the most. Their losses serve upon them a grave, as it were, injustice that cannot be explained.   In their grieving process, those who lose loved ones to drunk drivers go through an initial period during which they are just angry. I pass no judgment on them during this phase for they have and are entitled to a righteous indignation. Some move along from the anger phase into revenge. They attend the criminal proceedings. They call the lawyer who is representing them on a daily basis so that they can check on when they will see monetary justice. They want their pound of flesh.

But there's a remarkable group that moves beyond the anger into MADD. The MADD (Mothers Against Drunk Driving) group rises up, determined not to let their loved ones' lives be lost in vain. They do not want anyone else to face what they have. They become activists. They labor in the high schools, in rehab clinics, on prom nights, and in the courts. They will go anywhere to speak to anyone so that they can tell their stories. They are armed with pictures and warnings. They cope with their losses through service to society. Their healing comes through their dedication to a cause. With enough time I discovered that these loved ones who have been left with such a senseless void see their work in prevention as some answer to their "Why?"

I also see the transition. Those who morph into the MADD group are the ones you wouldn't pick from a pile of résumés. When I first met many of them, they were shy, distraught, and angry. That's a difficult combination for conversation. In those first meetings they just wanted somebody, anybody to just do something. They flail, they wail, and they agonize. They are also frequent visitors to the cemetery. But with each step toward activism, you see a part of them rise to the surface. A shy person would generally not take to public speaking. Yet they almost all end up in front of audiences as large as five hundred—just so they can be a voice of warning about alcohol. Some lobby for changes in laws, in everything from bar closing times to ID requirements for liquor sales. Others make prom night their special quest—getting the teens limos, rides, and supervised activities that keep them away from too much independence and alcohol. Amazingly, they sometimes have to get laws passed that make it a misdemeanor for parents to have parties for their teens where they serve, stunningly, alcohol.

The MADD folks lost loved ones, but they are reborn. Because of their love, they are willing to overcome their fears, their grief, and their taciturn ways to make a difference through their grief.

I saw my healing leap forward as I witnessed the MADD social activism. Because of their example, I began to think of ways to honor Claire. Knowing Claire, I can't imagine having buildings or scholarships in her name. She was so unassuming in life and so nondescript in death that even our bishop forgot to mention her death and funeral in church the Sunday after she died. Most people would take offense that their ecclesiastical leader forgot to bring up the death of one of the flock's members. But when I thought about it, I realized that his actions were perfectly consistent with Claire's life. Because of her disabilities, she was someone who caused averted eyes. Because of her disabilities, she spent a great deal of time at home with us and even at school she was in a classroom with only a few students. Some students at her high school did not even know there was a special ed classroom in their school let alone know of Claire. She had the patience to wait for her needs—others had to come to her because she could not summon them. Yet she was the strong bond of our family. She was the center of our schedules and our lives. She was the example of a quiet, reflective life.

Like my MADD friends, we needed a new direction, one of service, because we had to fill the void Claire's departure created. So dramatic was the change in our lives that weeks after Claire died, I was driving John home from school and there was a truck tailing us. I did not recognize the car, but John said, "That's Eric in his father's new truck, and Sam is with him." Even weeks after Claire's funeral I got angry and said, "Call him on his cell phone, John. If he's out riding around with Eric, he is in a lot of trouble because that means he left Claire at home alone!" John looked at me as if I were Miss Havershim. Claire was gone, but the habits of care were not. I had been so attuned and attentive for twenty years that it had become part of my DNA. And how I missed her needs. I missed the blessings of service to her. I missed her saintliness. We had lived with a soul who sought no worldly recognition. We had a perfect being in our home for nearly twenty years and then that blessing was taken. How do you rekindle the feeling that a divine spirit brings to your home?

The MADD folks helped me to realize that I need not leave that happy time behind. Claire was no longer with us, but she had taught us much and heightened our awareness of those with disabilities and the needs of those who care for them. We could seek out those who had Claire's celestial nature because of their physical and mental challenges.

My husband and I reactivated a foundation that my daughter Sarah and I began almost a decade ago. Our hope, with our Weaving Through the Maze Foundation, is to contribute money to provide assistance, respite care, and anything else we could think of to those families with chronically ill or disabled children. I saw the healing attributes of the activism that was my privilege to witness in the MADD cemetery folks. Our new task in life, indeed, a new lease on life, comes from returning to helping what we understand: what families with these perfect spirits need as they tend to their physical challenges. It had become interesting to me how many ideas and insights were born in my cemetery. "O, death, where is thy sting? O, grave, where is thy victory?"[84]

42

FUNERALS, FUNERAL STYLES, REVELATIONS, AND THE CROCK-POT

You can't help but notice the patterns. I did not keep charts and data, but it is clear that there are more funerals in January and February and again in July and August than during other times of the year. January and February are the cold and flu seasons, and we lose our fellow travelers at a more rapid pace. Those who have lived long lives and those who are under three are taken most frequently when viral plague besets us in the winter months.

July and August in Phoenix, Arizona, are rugged tests of endurance for the most physically fit. For our senior, senior citizens, the heat becomes a killer. We lose so many during the worst of summer. For those who tell us, "But it's a dry heat," I remind them that you still can't sit in an oven and survive.

You know the funerals are coming long before the hearse rolls in, along with the cars full of relatives. Rosencrantz and Guildenstern dig the graves first. When they dig the graves, their next step seems so stark—they cover the grave with a piece of plywood, as if the days of the pine box and pauper's field have returned. The plywood stays there until the day of the funeral. On that day, the awning, the green felt, the Astroturf ground covering, and the holder for the casket are all in place. All funeral setups are the same— same number of chairs, same green felt, same green Astroturf. You can never tell the station in life of the decedent from the funeral setup.

While the setup is the same, the funerals are not. I have seen funerals that involved two people, a casket, and a single rose. There is no religious figure, no words spoken, nothing. The goal is simply one of getting the casket in the ground. The sixteen chairs that have been set up are never used.

I have seen funerals that drew so many mourners that you couldn't get into the cemetery because of all the cars. These funerals are long and the many car drivers and occupants linger after the funeral.

I have seen Tongan funerals. The noise is something to behold. Folks who follow the Irish wake model just don't know what to do at or with a Tongan funeral. There is no such thing as a small Tongan funeral. Hundreds attend. Almost as many dance. Tongans throw a great send-off. Many other mourners are torn between morbid, as it were, curiosity and calling 9-1-1. "Are dancing Tongans allowed in the city cemetery?" That's the opening phrase in the 9-1-1 call. That would be a fun "Tape at 11" story for the local news.

Despite these wide variations in funeral processes, we still miss the point of a funeral. We fancy it to be a send-off, at least we do in our initial stages of grief. However, our friends' and loved ones' spirits are already gone and functioning elsewhere. The funeral is our deal. Call it closure. Call it a dose of reality. Call it one final tribute. Call it the opportunity to say what we wish we had said while they were still with us. The funeral is for us, the living.

Gaining this insight made me far more sensitive to the pressures our loved ones face when they will be in the position of throwing our funerals. I have given my children instructions with one theme: keep it simple. Use the funeral for closure, reality, whatever. But, use the funeral to begin healing. Ashes to ashes and dust to dust is all well and good, but, in the paraphrased words of the Monty Python boys, "I'm really not all that dead yet!" Despite my genealogy, I guess I'd like a little more Tongan and a little less Irish wake.

Closure is not the right word for a funeral. Funerals are beginnings for us, the loved ones. If we want to be with our friends and relatives who have begun the next phase of their lives, we need to start doing what we know we are supposed to be doing. My year of observing funerals brought me to this conclusion, "I have a perfect child who has gone on to the next life. I need to straighten up and fly right if I am going to be with her." I am quite certain I did not understand that at her funeral as I focused on my loss. But thanks to the Tongans, I have inched my way toward understanding, then belief, and then testimony that my daughter is quite fine. I have some work to do. The Tongan funerals are by no means quiet, but that quiet testimony has come to me over the course of 365-plus days.

So often, during my year of the graveyard, other parents would tell me about dreams of their children speaking to them. Others swore they saw their children sitting on their beds. When I heard these stories, I kept thinking, "What is wrong with me that I am not entitled to these miraculous revelations?" I came to understand that I had experienced a quieter miracle, a slow-cook, a Crock-Pot testimony. Elder Oaks explained this quiet growth: "Some [people] have looked exclusively for the great manifestations that are recorded in the scriptures and have failed to recognize the still, small voice that is given to them…We need to know that the Lord rarely speaks loudly. His messages almost always come in a whisper… Not understanding these principles of revelation, some people postpone acknowledging their testimony until they have experienced a miraculous event. They fail to realize that with most people…gaining a testimony is not an event but a process."[85] My process ran at a glacial pace and there was no sudden testimony that Claire lives. But I got there on Crock-Pot low.

43

DOUBLE-DECKERS AND NO FEAR

Some are six feet, and some are nine feet. Hang around a cemetery long enough and you notice that Rosencrantz and Guildenstern have different depths for graves. The nine-footers are what I call the double-deckers. These are the couple graves. Because of space constraints you no longer lie beside your companion, one of you goes in first, and the other tops off the grave. Terry and I bought the plot next to Claire's (who has the luxury of a single grave), and we have a double-decker. We wanted to be next to Claire. We also recognized the economy for grave visits by our children; they could catch everyone in one fell swoop.

However, the double-decker introduced a strange tension in our relationship. It's a bit like a *Maude* episode when Maude realizes that her husband, Walter, is not as selfless as she had assumed. Walter runs out of a burning theater without one iota of concern for Maude. With a double-decker, you start wondering, "Hey, who's going in first?" It's not a matter of wanting to know outcome. Once you have that double-decker, suspicion sets into daily life. I have accused Terry of taking too many liberties in making left turns when I am his passenger. As it turns out, suspicions sometimes have grounding. Following one close-call-of-a-left turn, I chastised Terry for risk and he explained, "I'm not going in on the bottom of that double-decker plot."

How ironic that two people who struggled with the undertaker now have this running joke about our demise, our grave (singular), and our remains. Because of my year at the cemetery, we have all the funeral issues out of the way. Spending so much time at a cemetery has stolen a great deal of death's thunder. Not sting, thunder. Terry says that once you have lost a child, your thoughts on death change completely. He's right. You eventually find your way to feeling as if you are in a win-win situation. If life marches on, you are here for your children, family, and friends. If your time comes, you know that you will be reunited with the darling daughter who left you too soon. Perspective is the yield from working your way past grief and into a position of losing death's grip. Do your worst, you are able to say aloud, with fist raised to the grim reaper. Because of perspective I see myself doing my best Scarlett O'Hara, eyes forward, feet firmly planted, "As God is my witness, I am not afraid." And I am not.

I have often wondered when I read stories of self-sacrifice what kind of person would give his or her life to help another. On January 13, 1982, a Boeing 737 crashed into the 14th Street Bridge in Washington, DC, after the pilot took off in a snowstorm. There would be seventy-eight people killed in the accident, including Arland D. Williams Jr., who kept giving the rescue helicopter's life preserver to other passengers in the water as the rescue workers, hobbled by weather, tried to save lives. There he floated in the freezing waters, always deferring, turning over the life preserver to others until he slipped quietly beneath the water. A clergyman said of Mr. Williams, "His heroism was not rash. Aware that his own strength was fading, he deliberately handed hope to someone else, and he did so repeatedly. On that cold and tragic day, Arland D. Williams Jr. exemplified one of the best attributes of human nature, specifically that some people are capable of doing 'anything' for total strangers."[86]

An essay in *Time* magazine described what Mr. Williams did with brilliant perspective: "If the man in the water gave a lifeline to the people gasping for survival, he was likewise giving a lifeline to those who observed him."[87] I am not sure I had developed the depth to completely understand this gentle hero until we lost Claire. Those who watch us from the side need to see strength, and, like Mr. Williams, I have come to understand that one way or the other, all is well. That's not just a conquest of grief, but it is also evidence of faith that borders on certainty. You no longer ask "What if?" You are ready with whenever.

44

MR. NAPKINHEAD AND THE WAVE

At first he seemed like one of my hallucinations. He had snow-white hair and a matching, lengthy beard. Then, because of obvious similarities, I thought that perhaps the chore of keeping a watchful eye at the cemetery was what Santa did during the off-season. Still, there he was, just as present each day around Christmas as he was in April. He walked the many streets of the cemetery each day. He always wore dark glasses, a hat, long sleeves, gloves— he was really covered with clothing from head to toes. A ZZ Top look for the later years.

At times I wasn't sure there was a face there. For all I know it could have been Mr. Napkinhead walking the cemetery. For months we seemed to stare at each other as I passed by him. I couldn't really say for sure if he was staring at me because of the dark glasses, but I knew his head was turned in my direction. How odd! Another thought that I had for months was that he may have been misdirected from a *NOTLD* sequel that ended with budget problems. So, I was leery of him.

Then one May morning I noted that Santa ZZ Napkinhead came to the cemetery in shorts. Everything else remained covered, but I saw his knees. Real flesh and blood. Safe zone—not a ghoul. The knees melted my heart. They were a whiter shade of pale, but they were knees nonetheless. When we did our ships-passing-in-the-cemetery routine, I couldn't help but smile at this sudden, bold change and sartorial splendor. When I smiled, Santa's arm went up in a wave. Oh, this was not your perfunctory, obligatory wave—this was the wave of an old friend, a really comfortable old friend and one you were just pleased to see. One smile, one wave, one bond between two souls who found that a cemetery is a fairly decent place to pay a visit each day.

Each day Santa and I exchanged a wave. His was bold and large. Mine, because of the limited space a Volvo offered, was smaller, but rapid, back and forth, like a puppy's tail. And I have just about the same feelings I imagine a puppy has when she sees someone who means a great deal to her. Santa and I did not speak because while his wave is large and friendly, he just keeps walking. I don't want to intrude on his walk, but he is my friend.

One must never assume. We judge, prejudge, conclude, and avoid. We are so often wrong in our assumptions about people based on the outward appearance. The Lord is much kinder to us. In chastising Samuel for making yet another mistake in assessing individuals by outward appearance (first Saul, and then Eliab), the Lord explains, "Look not on his countenance, or on the height of his stature; because I have refused him: for the Lord seeth not as man seeth; for man looketh on the outward appearance, but the Lord looketh on the heart." [88] I had judged on everything but the heart when I first saw Santa Napkinhead.

Once I got past the judgment, I found a constancy in Santa's presence. He played a role in my recovery through his unfailing appearances, with all their color and charm. I have since learned from others that Santa is ill, with a slew of ailments, but he says that the exercise makes him feel better and that the cemetery is a safe and quiet place to walk. Except for an occasional road-rage incident postfuneral, he's right. With all of his illnesses, none of which carries a positive prognosis, Santa remains observant and considerate. He has struggles and pains I can't imagine, but he reached out to me with a wave that said, "Ain't life great!" What an odd message to find in a cemetery. And I am grateful I happened to be there for his instruction.

45

ROLLING ATTENTION IN HISTORIC CEMETERIES

Claire's grave is located in a new section of the cemetery. It will be the final section of the Mesa Cemetery because there is no more available land for expansion. I guess Henny Youngman would sum it up, "People are dying to get in here." Claire's place will soon be closed. "Once it is filled," the librarian-voiced office manager for the cemetery explained, "this will become a historic cemetery." "Filled" seemed like an odd word to describe a cemetery with no more room. "Filled" is a word that goes with sippy cups and toddlers, hoses and swimming pools, Krispy Kreme donuts and crème. Wouldn't "fully occupied" be better? "No vacancies?" "Once Phase I sells out?" We needed something here with at least some subdivision lingo that would convey the concept of limited turf.

When Claire was buried, her grave was one of only seven in the new and final section. It was a lonesome place in the early days, but the neighbors have arrived. The new section of the cemetery now looks like a field of flowers as you drive toward it. Many have joined Claire in this final section. The new section is busier than the long-occupied portions of the cemetery. There are more visitors. I have thought about the lack of visitors in the older portions of the cemetery and wondered if there are fewer visitors because with the passage of time, the grief is conquered, the longing ends, and the living find other things to do.

But, in exploring the cemetery from its initial phase through to this final plot sellout, I have discovered a natural order. Those who left us in the 1800s rest in Phase I, their children then rest in Phase II, their grandchildren rest in Phase III. Generations move through cemeteries. For the most part, people seem to live long lives, following the natural order. They buy their burial plots when they need them—advance purchases are odd to most folks. So, there is a time line that runs through the cemetery. Enter on the older east side and you find little activity. As you drive through, the flowers, visitors, and activity increase.

Like a wave going through a crowd at a football game, the time passes for each group. One group sits down, and the next group rises. Eventually they will all be resting—at least until the Resurrection and then we will have another form of the wave if Revelations is correct on the Second Coming and the dead rising.

For now, the initial occupants have fewer visitors because their children and grandchildren have joined them; they are just residing down the road a bit. Claire's neighbors, who were in their 90s when they passed away, are the grandchildren of those who took up residence in the 1800s. All cemeteries are historic. Even without the visitors and the flowers, markers and tombstones remain in perpetuity and history abounds.

A cemetery is a story of lives. Another epiphany. No one escapes without passing into the next life. I took consolation in knowing that there were many who had gone before and many more to come. It all seemed so very natural, so historic, and so promising in that we will all have the same capstone experience that nets us, well, a capstone in the form of a tombstone. This realization of this orderly process of death made grieving easier because it just keeps going, and in a regimented fashion. There is a plan! You can just see it laid out in a cemetery if you study it enough.

The somehow calming effect of the rolling cemetery phenomenon was an answer to questions, a reassurance during grieving, and insight in a period of confusion. Elder David Bednar noted that even the Prophet Joseph Smith got his answer in piecemeal fashion, and that we should expect the same. Not all answers come all at once in a singular experience in a sacred grove.[89] I found reassurance in the talk he gave on this concept at BYU–Idaho in

2001. In that talk he said that he and Sister Bednar knew each other for nineteen months and then dated for fifteen months before they were married These are my kind of people—I had spent somewhere between fifteen and nineteen months at the cemetery. Elder Bednar explained, "I do not recall ever receiving a single, overwhelming spiritual confirmation that she was 'the one.' I do recall that as we dated, as we talked, as we became better acquainted, and as we observed and learned about each other in a variety of circumstances, I received many small, simple, and quiet reassurances that she was indeed a remarkable and spiritual woman. All of those simple answers over a period of time led to and produced an appropriate spiritual reassurance that indeed we were to be married."[90]

Things come to us as "the dews from heaven."[91] President Joseph F. Smith spoke of the dangers of signs, miracles, and visions: "Show me Latter-day Saints who have to feed upon miracles, signs and visions in order to keep them steadfast in the Church, and I will show you members...who are not in good standing before God, and who are walking in slippery paths. It is not by marvelous manifestations unto us that we shall be established in the truth, but it is by humility and faithful obedience to the commandments and laws of God."[92] I'll take dew.

46

THE DECORATIONS

I glanced over at a headstone of a young man who was killed on his motorcycle. There were flowers on his headstone, but someone had also carefully placed a can of Bud Light near those flowers. A trucker rests in peace near Claire and someone often comes and places a pack of Marlboros on his headstone. On occasion I see a can of 7UP, a 7-Eleven Slurpee, or Circle K Thirst Buster on graves here and there. Model trucks and ATVs are also popular choices. Everyone grieves in different ways, and they also decorate the graves of loved ones in everything from nouveau clutter to holiday themes.

Some folks make sure that the hobbies of their dear departeds are known. They put carvings in the markers and headstones to show what their loved ones enjoyed doing. The grave of a twenty-year-old young man has a four-wheel ATV carved on the left side. The trucker has a big-rig fourteen-wheeler carved on his headstone. There are many jumping fish and fishing rods on quite a few of the male occupants' tombstones. Feminism has not yet brought women around to the angler thing. Women have flowers, hearts, and temples carved on their headstones. Men have hobbies and vehicles carved on theirs.

Some folks simply maintain the graves of their loved ones. They plant grass, put down Astroturf, fertilize, water, and hope that their loved one's grave looks better than any other. They don't decorate; they farm.

The Boys Scouts join us in decorating for Presidents' Day, Memorial Day, July 4, Veterans Day, and Christmas. Flags go up on the first four and wreaths land in for Christmas.

Some families decorate for every holiday. I was stunned to see ghosts, bats, pumpkins, and Draculas adorning the graves of many during October. Flashing lights appear for Halloween and Christmas. Christmas finds moving trains, three-foot-tall candy canes, Santas, sleighs, snow, North Pole signs, and picket fences—and these are just the adult's graves. There is some ongoing competition for the size of Christmas trees placed on graves. From three inches to four feet, you can find any size you like.

My favorite grave was one located a football field away from Claire. Each holiday, whoever was in charge took the full six-by-three-foot area to put up cobwebs, rotating reindeer pulling a Santa sleigh, Easter bunnies hopping, and colored eggs hanging from a nearby tree. I watched in wonder over the course of a year at the extent of effort and expense in decorating the grave. My initial reaction from afar was that it had to be the grave of a child. However, the grave was clearly in a Phase III development section and nowhere near the baby section.

Eventually, curiosity and the dancing gourds at Thanksgiving got to me. I walked over to see the grave marker. Therein, resting in peace, was a Hells Angels biker. Mom was the decorator extraordinaire. I have visions of him looking down from biker heaven and exclaiming, "For crying out loud, Mom, what will the guys think?"

That there is whimsy at the cemetery was, at once, reassuring to me, but troubling. Perhaps the decorating projects put misplaced importance on their death and distracted from our lives. C. S. Lewis envisions that the dead are on the other side begging us to stop our mourning. While he passes no judgment on those who visit, decorate, and police their loved ones' graves ("I'd better keep my breath to cool my own porridge"), he does wonder if perhaps we are going in circles when we "emphasize their deadness."[93] Robert C. Ingersoll, in addition to his insights that ended up on Woody Hayes's headstone, also thought that every headstone should be engraved with the phrase, "I really am better now." I believe he meant the phrase to describe with reassurance the condition of our loved ones who have ended the earthly phase of their lives. They want us to move forward! Oh, but, those holidays are a struggle.

47

THE FIRST CHRISTMAS

A friend who lost his wife warned me when Claire died that the "year of firsts" would be difficult. He explained that we all must go through the first Thanksgiving, the first Christmas, the first birthday without our departed loved one. The grief, however controlled, percolates to the surface, as it should. Holidays are a time when families gather and memories are made. How could we not feel their presence acutely?

So, I knew, from my dear friend's warning, that these holidays would be tense. The first Christmas after Claire died, I had no decorations. I didn't put my Snow Village out, and I put up a tree on December 24, with lights only, no decorations. No wreath on the door—nothing. That first Christmas after Claire died found me calling one of my sisters on December 5 and saying, "I knew it was going to be bad, but I didn't think it would be this bad this early."

I plotted a strategy, something that Mr. Carlin on the old *Bob Newhart Show* devised to get through the holidays. He planned to stay awake for two days prior to Thanksgiving, Christmas, and Easter with the goal of sleeping through the actual holiday so that he didn't feel the pain of being alone that accompanies those who are narcissistic, paranoid boors. Mr. Carlin also added that he wasn't sure his plan would work all that well for Lent.

I continued to dread Christmas Eve and Christmas itself. How, oh, how, I fretted, would I get through? Christmas was a double whammy for us because Claire's final illness began just three days after the last Christmas we had with her. Not only were we facing Christmas, we were coming up on the one-year mark.

Some folks opt to spend that first Christmas in a way that does not allow the memories to creep in and salt the grief wounds that they have managed to begin healing. In *Ordinary People*, Mary Tyler Moore, in an uncharacteristically cold role, wanted to spend Christmas in London after she and Donald Sutherland lost their son in a boating accident. We came close to running away. But we stayed, battened down the hatches, and weathered that first Christmas in our own home as we had every other Christmas. Save one thing—Christmas morning was different. I have always stepped outside early on Christmas morning to feel the silence. There is no other morning like it. Step outside early and you hear nothing. No cars, for everyone is in their homes. No dogs, for they have been invited in for the family festivities. There's the same silence you feel when you stand in a field when the snow has filled it. Snow insulates and silence is a natural result. Silence and I were friends long before Claire took up residence in the quietest real estate we have here on earth.

So I stepped outside that first Christmas morning and took in the silence. Then it hit me—if it's this quiet here… And so I disturbed others' Christmas morning silence and drove to the cemetery. Claire and I were alone there that morning. It was no different from any other Christmas morning in the previous nineteen years. Claire and I were always the first ones awake, and just the two of us would enjoy the silence of the house and the stillness of the outdoors on Christmas morning. There we were, the two of us alone together again, just in a different setting.

In the silence of the morning in that cemetery that had only one living visitor, I was reminded of the day's importance. We mark the birth of the Savior, someone who has given us a guarantee that Claire lives on. I left the cemetery a C. S. Lewis convert—emphasize the living. I went home to roust the household, toss a few decorations on the tree, and experience the joy that Christmas brings in its promises. I had made it through another "first" and even talk about it. I can't say there were not tears that morning, but there was some semblance of normalcy and a great deal of assurance that comes from faith and a refocus on why Christmas exists.

That morning I had lived through something David Hales described: "Suffering is universal; how we react to suffering is individual. Suffering can take us one of two ways. It can be a strengthening and purifying experience combined with faith, or it can be a destructive force in our lives if we do not have the faith in the Lord's atoning sacrifice. The purpose of suffering, however, is to build and strengthen us. We learn obedience by the things we suffer."[94] What I had been learning at the cemetery was how to react to our loss of Claire, and not focus on the suffering. In short, perhaps our Claire was offering a big, "Move along, folks. Nothing to see here."

48

THE ONE-YEAR MARK

The ultimate first is the first anniversary (if that's what you can call such an occasion) of the death.

I was also warned by my friend that the one-year mark would be a dark time. I didn't understand what he meant—until the one-year mark arrived. In many ways, the one-year mark is worse than the actual death. At least at the time of death, you have the blessing of being in shock, handling the strain of funeral arrangements, and working through the sheer logistics of relatives and friends throughout the house. At the one-year mark, you are sane and not consumed with details. At the one-year mark, you realize that death is a permanent state (at least until the Resurrection). That's a tough pill to swallow.

But, I had made so much progress, and so many wonderful experiences that I couldn't see how the marking of the first year would be so difficult. But, despite all the progress, I can only say that the pain at the time of that first-year mark is acute. I understand why too. The one-year mark is Satan's one last shot at discouragement, at winning you over on the grounds of unfairness, injustice, and "Why me?" Satan works the hardest when he knows he faces a turning-point battle. The one-year mark is that turning point.

We sometimes fail to see how incredibly clever Satan can be. Ernest LeRoy Hatch, the former president of the Guatemala City Temple, once said, "The devil is not smart because he is the devil; he is smart because he is old."[95] We are warned repeatedly by our leaders to be careful of Satan's cunning, his persuasive and enticing speech, and his increased activity when he perceives he is losing ground. Because of my experiences at the cemetery, he had lost ground on the tool of discouragement. He was using the one-year reminder to strike during vulnerability. If you are not careful, Satan makes sense. President James Faust wrote, "Who has not heard and felt the enticing of the devil? His voice often sounds so reasonable and his message so easy to justify. It is an appealing, intriguing voice with dulcet tones. It is neither hard nor discordant. No one would listen to Satan's voice if it sounded harsh or mean. If the devil's voice were unpleasant, it would not persuade people to listen to it."[96] President Faust also said that he recalled sixty years earlier when he nearly fell into Satan's trap, a trap that would have derailed him of his life's work and role in the Church. If apostles have vulnerability, where did I stand on the one-year mark of my daughter's death?

At the one-year mark, I came as close as I ever have to losing my faith. It felt like an out-of-body, R.E.M. song experience: "That's me in the corner. That's me in the spotlight, losing my religion." I also had a great many unhelpful platitudes tossed my way by those who had never lost a child, to wit, "They are only ours temporarily. We get to care for them, but they can be taken at any time." I hated that common offering. Some who offered this form of reassurance had between six and eight children. Children had not come easily to Terry and me. We had spent thousands and pushed medical science to the limits to get the five children we had, two of which we lost. I was clearly going the wrong direction in terms of amassing a family. One child lost to a late miscarriage and another lost at nearly age 20. And here were people with eight children telling me my children are only loaners, and the lease (bailment?) can expire at any time.

The one-year mark following Claire's death was a dark period, almost as if I could feel the adversary's tug. Elder Holland described the power of Satan in his devotional address:

'...trouble has no necessary connection with discouragement—discouragement has a germ of its own, as different from trouble as arthritis is different from a stiff joint' (*The Crack-Up,* ed. Edmund Wilson, New

York: James Laughlin, 1945, p. 77). Troubles we have all got, but the 'germ' of discouragement, to use Fitzgerald's word, is not in the trouble, it is in us—or to be more precise, I believe it is in Satan, the prince of darkness, the father of lies. And he would have it be in us. It's frequently a small germ, hardly worth going to the Health Center for, but it will work and it will grow and it will spread. In fact it can become almost a habit, a way of living and thinking, and there the greatest damage is done. Then it takes an increasingly severe toll on our spirit, for it erodes the deepest religious commitments we can make—those of faith, and hope, and charity. We turn inward and look downward, and these greatest of Christlike virtues are damaged or at very least impaired. We become unhappy and soon make others unhappy, and before long Lucifer laughs.[97]

Clearly, I was looking down, and I could feel Satan's grip through discouragement. During this dark one-year period, a woman in our ward who just had her seventh child stood in testimony meeting and said that each time she passed the hospital where her seventh child was born she found that she burst into tears of joy because giving birth was such a spiritual experience. All I could think of was that each time I pass a hospital I think of Claire being there. I see her intubated. I recall the sleepless nights, the vigils, and the feeling that there was nothing more we could do. The contrast was too much—her joy and seven healthy children even as I dealt with my one-year mark sans another child.

I have never begrudged others their healthy children and picture-perfect lives. I admire them and am happy that their lives have unfolded without harm to their children. I only wish them the best. But Satan is a master at using comparison and perceived injustice in a way that causes that bitterness to creep in. Shakespeare warned, "The prince of darkness is a gentleman," and it seemed as if his appeal to me was protecting me from the harshness of our loss.[98] From bitterness springs resentment and then anger. The natural result of these negative feelings is a desire to pull away from spirituality because Satan has convinced you that you are entitled to all these feelings of resentment, anger, and injustice.

So, I left church after the seven-time mother's testimony, got home, and had the body sobs. By this time, those in my immediate family had moved on. My husband and sons seemed immune to sadness. They did not experience the one-year trauma as I did. They did not follow me home to see if I was okay. Just as well; I probably would have questioned their lack of feeling in not reacting to someone experiencing joy in seeing a hospital.

In the midst of this wallowing, the thought came, "Go to the cemetery." I had never been to the cemetery on Sunday at that time of day—I was always in church. I didn't want to go—I just wanted to continue being angry at happy people who had *all* of their children. The prompting to go was too strong, so I succumbed.

When I arrived at the cemetery, there was Grace. We spoke at almost the same time, "I never come at this time, and here you are." We both recognized a blessing, some kind of an intervention to lift me from a downward spiral. Another hug came quickly. Grace saw my tears, and this time she was strong for me as I had been for her when we first met nearly a year before. I explained why I was there and Grace said, "They just don't understand." But Grace did. Cemetery friends. We help them and they help us. As Grace said, "When I was down you were strong. Now you're down, and I can be strong for you."

The doubts about my faith dissipated because I realized that we can't always get what we want. Mick Jagger is not a spiritual type, but he finished the thought for me that day in the cemetery. We can't always get what we want, but we do get what we need. I wanted Claire, I lost Claire, but I got Grace. Grace and I agreed that it was more than sheer chance that found us together there at our times of despair. He sends us help, through people, through humor, and through the quiet still of the cemetery. I regained my faith that morning as Grace and I walked and talked. Gratitude replaced grief. Faith replaced despair. Grace was the angel who was right on time.

As I drove away from the cemetery that day, my beloved classic rock-and-roll station was still tuned on my radio. Someone in our church said that her husband had seven hundred hymns on his iPod and that's what he listens to. I felt very small because, unless you count Led Zeppelin's "Stairway to Heaven" as a hymn, I was, at that time, hymnless, on my iPod. I was playing my classic rock station because I was still angry about the joyful people. It is funny how the Comforter finds a way to get through even on our terms and despite our music. As I drove from the cemetery that Sunday morning, Iron Butterfly's *In-a-Gadda-Da-Vida,* the long version, came on. This was the song that always came on during the Saturday night drives I often had with Claire. "Here comes the drum solo, Claire" was what I used to warn. And I would tap her tiny fingers to those drums. She would get a funny look when the squeaking guitars started. It may have been the only truly teenage thing Claire ever did. She questioned her parents' sanity and taste in music during the 1960s.

How Claire and I enjoyed Iron Butterfly's musical stylings! What are the chances I would hear that song at that moment? The only thing that could have made it any better is if the purple flame wagon and/or unicyclist had drifted by. I half expected them that morning. I have been so spoiled by all the attention I have been given to help me with this thing called grief.

I regained my religion, but I daresay I never lost it. I was wallowing a bit and needed a little boost to regain all the progress I had made over the past year. Paul's second letter to the Corinthians offers reassurance: "For our light affliction, which is but for a moment, worketh for us a far more exceeding and eternal weight of glory."[99] Grace, Iron Butterfly, and the cemetery gave me an appreciation of how attuned our Heavenly Father is to us at our low points. That day, He even got through the anger, the bitterness, and the truly bad music. He cannot always change nature's course on illnesses, but He will not abandon us. Indeed, there is no limit to the ways He finds and the people He uses to see us through the rough patches. Elder Holland said, "Some disappointments come regardless of your effort and preparation, for God wishes us to be strong as well as good."[100] I had trouble with both "strong" and "good" that day, but our Heavenly Father got through on the message channels I chose in defiance that day.

49

EASING THE ONE-YEAR MARK FOR OTHERS

Because I had reached my one-year mark and lived to tell about it, I developed a heightened sensitivity to its significance and its pain. I marked the one-year "anniversaries" of all my cemetery friends' loved ones on my calendar. As their one-year marks approached, I sent a card to those whose address I had. For those I did not know as well, I left cards on the headstones sealed in Ziploc bags and taped to the headstones. I wanted them to know that I was keenly aware of what they were facing.

They all took the time to write a thank-you note to me. "Someone remembered!" "Someone cares!" I found notes back from them on Claire's headstone. They were touched, but I helped myself more than I had helped them. I was able to worry about someone else. Having lived through the one-year mark, I did not want them to be alone. For someone who did well to catch living relatives' birthdays, it was a miracle for me to timely send these one-year notes. One card and note from a mother and father who had suddenly lost their thirty-year-old son said it best: "Only we who have lost a child truly can understand." And we understand the one-year mark as well.

After the one-year mark, you don't see your cemetery friends as often. We do find our ways back to regular life. But, for eternity, regardless of how many times we would see each other, I had my cemetery friends and they had me. I imagine that corporations pay good money to consultants to deliver on intense bonding experiences that make employees be team players. The theory of the expensive consultants who deliver *Survivor* type experiences for employees is that you develop a close relationship (at least as much as federal antiharassment laws allow) that binds you together just because you survived.

My cemetery friends are my *Survivor* team members. I owe them for strength and for allowing me to be a part of their healing as they were part of mine.

50

THE CEMETERY NETS AN EAGLE PROJECT AND POLICE INTERROGATION

The following sentence is one I never could have imagined I would write: going to the cemetery each day got John, my youngest son, an Eagle project. Now there's a miracle.

Saturdays are busy days at the cemetery. Lots of funerals, lots of visitors, and, on occasion, groups of people who look like they just came from a ward pancake breakfast. I asked Rick why I had seen hardworking civilians in the cemetery one Saturday. He explained that the staff allotted for the cemetery is just enough for funeral preparations and maintenance. The big projects are always deferred because of manpower. He said he has his wish list and that he hopes that Eagle Scout candidates come along and offer to help.

Oh, you dear man, said I! I have a Life Scout in search of a project. Rick asked if my son John could take a historic section of the cemetery and find, raise, and paint the hub markers. Hub markers are like survey markers. Every grave is aligned with the markers. "The problem is," Rick explained, "that with irrigation, grass, and mowing, a good portion of them have disappeared. We don't have the staff to go through and do this, so each time we need to dig a grave, we have to search and find the markers."

With some donated Home Depot marker flags, some Ace Hardware spray paint, and a metal detector, Terry, John, three of his friends, and I spent five hours searching for markers and planting a Home Depot flag of conquest each time we located one. In this Phase I of the great cemetery Eagle Scout project, Rick had forgotten to let the park police know we would be working in the cemetery. A woman visiting the cemetery saw the six of us out there with a metal detector in the cemetery and called the police. The police arrived even as the woman stood guard from her car—to be certain these grave robbers did not flee. There is nothing like a police interrogation during an Eagle Scout project; you have a nice flavor to the write-up, especially the portion of the report that requires these young men to discuss what they would do differently. We and our metal detector were, however, released on our own recognizance.

Having escaped arrest the previous evening, we six rogues returned the next day with thirty adults and Scouts and set them loose to dig, raise, and paint. Those who helped us called it one of the best Eagle projects they had ever done. I found the boys and adults alike stopping to study the headstones. The dates on the headstones and the stories they imagined told me that they too were taken with the lives of their kindred dead. The hearts of the children were again turned.

After everyone had left, Terry, John, and I walked the section of the cemetery we had just repaired to be sure we had not missed any hub marker. As we walked, my waving friend, Santa, stopped to commend us. He spoke to me, "I know you. I've seen you here a lot." Indeed. He added that he had witnessed the police interrogation the evening before and was about to come to my rescue to vouch for me: "I knew exactly what you were doing. It's nice that you care about this place. My walks here have kept me going." Dear, Santa, I know the feeling.

51

MY CEMETERY FRIENDS HEAL, AND SO DO I

It was somewhere around eighteen months that I was able to be at home and not go to the cemetery. As Rick told me, it was a natural transition. I knew when it was time.

I no longer go to the cemetery each day, but the cemetery is a dear, old friend. You don't just abandon an old friend. But once that transition was made, the cemetery and I are on different terms. When I visit I recall the healing process and all the experiences I had among the headstones. It is rare when I see a member of our old gang, that gang of parents and grandparents who lost children and grandchildren in the same one-year period. On occasion there is another funeral. I find the newly bereaved are drawn to me, and I continue to help. Perhaps I am known as the cemetery's resident hugger.

When I come to the cemetery, Rick, Rosencrantz, and Guildenstern wave. One time near Christmas, I neglected to give a big enough wave to one of my friends. The next time I visited, he asked if anything was wrong because my wave wasn't friendly enough. I love that I mean something to those who care for Claire's memorial and the marvelous Ritz-Carlton facilities in which her remains rest. "For they that be with us are more than they that be with them."[101]

Everyone grieves differently, but time, silence, a cemetery, and helping others proved to be the tools for healing. I don't believe any parent ever really gets over the loss of a child. But you do learn to live with it. Even better, you learn about yourself, life, blessings, and priorities. Eventually you achieve a serenity that is quite nearly as calming as the cemetery on one of those mornings following a holiday. Everyone does their duty the day before, and you are alone. Alone with the memory of a magnificent soul who left you too early but stayed with you in spirit until she was sure you were healed. And I am.

Just as Rick predicted, time would heal all of us, and those who used the cemetery for healing would know when it was their time. It was their time to move along. Having had so many cemetery friends, I have seen this transformation up close and personal. There comes a time in each of their lives when they can no longer depend on this support group among the headstones. They understand that they are rejoining life's mainstream, a locale that does not carry many folks past, and certainly not into, the cemetery.

I saw Grace's transformation so vividly. Her countenance changed when she reached her point of healing. As noted, Alicia was an organ donor. One year after Alicia died, Grace was invited to a gathering for transplant donees and the relatives of the donors. Grace said she was initially hesitant to go, but she gathered her gumption and attended. She met a young boy who had received one of Alicia's kidneys. His mother could not stop thanking Grace. As they spoke, Grace said she watched the young man and he seemed to be twirling and dancing. "Has he always been this good of a dancer?" was Grace's question to his mother. "Oh, no. That just started after the transplant." Alicia was a wonderful dancer and, as a child, used to say to Grace, "Mommy, watch me twirl." Grace knew that Alicia lives on in so many ways. Grace had a new dignity and happiness about her.

Brenda and Bill have traveled and helped care for Alex's younger brother. Their daughter Rachel had a third child, a little girl, just three months shy of the second-year mark for Alex's passing. Brenda continues to e-mail me to share pictures of this glorious family, and she always ends with, "God is good." When Brenda visits the cemetery, she will often leave a note on

Claire's grave, "I felt Claire's presence here so strongly." She worked to help see me through a tough 365-plus days.

My friends are there on the same days as others—Memorial Day, Christmas, Thanksgiving. On Mother's Day Grace sewed us all silk roses and placed them on the graves of our children. As a result, I don't see my cemetery friends as often now. Time heals, just as Jefferson said. But I recognize that even in her death Claire managed to teach me, mold me, and comfort me. I have been to college and graduate school and have a career that spans nearly four decades now. But the total of all those years of education and experience never brought me the insight given so freely by my cemetery and cemetery friends. I was humbled. I was trained. I was helped. And it was very clear that I was loved, here on earth and from heaven.

C. S. Lewis wrote that sorrow is not a state, but a process, and it therefore needs not a map, but a history. I have a history of my 365-plus days at the cemetery that show not a sudden healing, but a transition. We never know the exact day that spring arrives, but we do look around one day and see the buds on the trees. There was no one day, one event, or one insight that transformed me, but with each day I inched a little closer toward spring. I think of Claire every day. I go to the cemetery about once each week. I go because I am reminded of the process, the effort, and the time I invested to heal.

I miss my Claire. I will always miss my Claire. I am not entirely convinced a parent ever truly recovers from the loss of a child, but I do believe we learn to cope with it and are able to gain that blessed assurance that they are well. Indeed, I have found my way back to the shore with such strength that I can abide the platitudes I hear from those who have not lost a child. I learned the skill of reflection at the cemetery and the healing point I came to was a message from my Heavenly Father, the same one that C. S. Lewis found: "Now get on with it. Become a god."[102] "Get on with it!"[103] I have.

52

THE PONIES, EZEKIEL, ABBOTT AND COSTELLO, AND MISS HAVISHAM

In all the experiences, stories, and phases of the year or so of grieving, there was one overarching question that made its way into my prayers: "What am I supposed to be learning from all of this pain?" You have read much of what I learned, but there was one more thing. I was a little hard on Ezekiel. When our leaders say, "Study the scriptures," they really do mean study—each word. Think back to what Ezekiel wrote. Initially, I interpreted that to mean that the man just went about his daily life as if nothing had happened. Actually, what Ezekiel wrote was that after his wife died that evening, "I did in the morning as I was commanded." I envisioned Ezekiel as callous, just moving right along from the loss of his beloved. No, a careful read tells us that Ezekiel just did in the morning what he was commanded to do. There is a difference. Following the commandments is the remedy for grief. So, I drift back and forth between Miss Havisham and Job, Ezekiel and Abbott and Costello, but there is always an eye focused on doing what I am supposed to be doing.

And I have found new strength in the stories of lives that do not always unfold ideally. We want to have a linear life—one that clicks along neatly in straight order, without all the mess of detours, tributaries, and out-and-out squiggles. Champions do not spring the linear life. Rather they are made champions through their nonlinear experiences.

There was one day at the cemetery when I was struck by the flowers on a grave that had just seen its funeral that day. One of the flower arrangements appeared to be in the shape of a horseshoe. You see that at Hialeah and other racetracks, but it seemed an odd arrangement for a funeral. I hoped that there would be some hint when the stone marker appeared, but, alas, nothing. You have to chuckle at a horse-race wreath making its way to a graveyard interment.

The irony about the experience is that I love the ponies. I follow the ponies. I've never placed a bet in my life, but I never miss watching the Triple Crown each year. The reason I follow the ponies is because behind every great racehorse there is a story that would have predicted they would never achieve the successes that would be theirs. The backdrop of champion horses from birth to win is always messy and challenging. Secretariat, often called the greatest racehorse of all time, was passed over in a coin toss before he was born. He ate as much as twopregnant mares. In one of his first races, his jockey rode injured. His owner, Penny Tweedy, lost her mother shortly before Secretariat was born, followed a few years later by her father's passing. She juggled managing her father's nearly bankrupt farm in Virginia with raising her family in Colorado. Secretariat captured the Triple Crown, winning the third and final race of that series by thirty-one lengths.

Seabiscuit's owner's son was killed in a tragic truck accident. Seabiscuit seemed too small to compete, his jockey seemed too heavy to be a jockey, and his trainer had been living as a hobo before he was hired to work with this unlikely champion. The horse captured the nation during the depression to lift the spirits of the "little guy."

In this year's Kentucky Derby, the original jockey of Animal Kingdom (the winner) was injured just before the race and had to be replaced. The third-place winner at the Derby this year, Mucho Macho Man, was believed to have been stillborn. As his owner and family mourned the lifeless foal, Mucho Macho Man got up and walked. His trainer, Kathy Ritvo, feels a kinship because she nearly died awaiting a heart transplant. A donor heart came through and she became the trainer for the miracle foal.

But my favorite pony story is that of Barbaro, the Triple Crown contender who died. Barbaro won the Kentucky Derby in May 2006 by six lengths. He went on to the Preakness, favored to win, but broke his leg after a false start. His jockey, Edgar Prado, dismounted and stood by the champion to hold him up until help could arrive. A racehorse cannot stand on three legs—this was a life-threatening injury. However, his owners, Roy and Gretchen Jackson, opted not to euthanize the horse. Barbaro traveled from Baltimore to the University of Pennsylvania in a caravan that found fans cheering along the route. Barbaro appeared to be a miracle horse after the surgery—he jogged to his stall once the anesthesia's effects were finished. Barbaro's treatment and recovery provided the means for surgeons at the university to techniques that have even translated to humans. Barbaro was a charmer with stamina who captured our hearts with his willingness to fight. From mid-May through December, he had five surgeries and still kept standing.

However, on the same day our Claire went into intensive care, in January 2007, Barbaro, because of a series of infections, had yet another surgery. Following yet another surgery on January 10, he was no longer able to stand. Claire passed away on January 11, 2007. Barbaro was euthanized because of his pain on January 29, 2007.

Such a tragedy to lose such strong spirits! Barbaro couldn't run his races. Claire never did run. So, we wonder, why? We see injustice when these innocent and fighting spirits are taken from us. But they are never taken from us—they are with us and they live on with their stories that give us strength. No champion has ever succeeded through an easy path. Indeed, the champion emerges because of the challenges.

So it is with that greatest challenge to our faith—the loss of our loved ones. We have but two choices: we can let the sorrow consume us, or we can go forward, honoring their legacy and making certain that their stories are told. Strength comes not in winning or in getting what we want as the outcome, but from the difficult path to understanding and accepting an outcome we would not have chosen. I would prefer to have our Claire with us, but I have found solace and strength in understanding why she is not.

The Afterword Preface: Of Funerals and Laying to Rest: Let Me Be Your
"Dot"
Don't Read This Until You Have Read Some Essays
Translation: This Is Not for the Faint-Hearted

This book has its preface after the book because, well, what follows
would be, as the young folks say, "way harsh" for starting off a book.
However, if you read the first few essays, you would be able to understand
this afterword and the purpose of the book.

There must be some book somewhere that prepares you for funeral
homes. Perhaps *Caskets and Vaults for Dummies*? Most people will endure
the silky, sullen tones of the undertaker and all of his questions and advice
when their parents, all in the natural order of things, pass on to the next
life. When they endure the tour of the casket room at that time, they will
have the distraction of brothers and sisters arguing over everything from
the color of the casket lining to the postfuneral luncheon scalloped pota-
toes. But when parents undertake, as it were, that gloomy task of funeral
arrangements for a child, they endure a game of solitaire with no hand-
book. Help is not forthcoming because the loss of a child is unspeakable.
We know how to pitch in when an octogenarian leaves us. But a child of
nineteen who has left us breaks protocol, and those natural instincts to lend
a hand at the hallowed halls of interment are just not there for those occasions. Losing a child is a parent's worst fear. Hanging around with parents
who have lost a child is awkward at best for most folks. The loss of the child
is hit one; the undertaker duties give you your sacking.

So, isolated parents muddle through the morbid task of casket selection
and vault pros and cons. But even after you've managed to waddle through
the dilemmas of "to have or not to have a police escort to the cemetery"
and the size, color, and design of the funeral program, you are not done.
The whole mortuary process actually takes a turn for the worse once you've
made all those decisions. That turn comes with a combination of words
I never imagined I would hear in a lifetime: "Mr. and Mrs. Jennings, I
need your signed permission to embalm your daughter." There better be
an undertaker with a voice for radio to break that kind of signed-release-
request to a set of parents. The nausea I felt that day comes back each time
those words flash through my mind, a somewhat regular event during the
first year after a death of a child. The regulator or consumer advocate who
came up with this requirement—that undertakers must obtain permission

from the next of kin for embalming the deceased—should be sentenced to making funeral lunches for families of three hundred. This sentence should apply throughout eternity. However, I believe there may be a natural statute of limitations here that would end their luncheon sentence when the millennium comes marching in (see Revelations). If the US Supreme Court does not strike down the undertakers' sentence as cruel and unusual in this life, and Revelations holds fast to its promises, we can give the undertakers a reprieve at that time. Who needs undertakers and funeral lunches when death has lost its sting?

We rarely speak of last breaths and the logistics of burial. These are verboten subjects, something that seems so odd given the inevitability of dealing with both. Because we have social norms that preclude discussion, I was not prepared for the haunting effect of the funeral home questions and processes. The process of grieving includes not only the flashes of those last moments of life, but it brings the traumatic experience of being forced to make rational and time-sensitive decisions when the gaping wound of your loss has not even been dressed. Undertakers give you one more experience that will flash through your mind and one more burden to try and shelve. They are good people, but they offer salt to the wound.

Oddly, in the midst of that embalming day experience, the beginning of a key healing process for conquering grief emerged. After the lovely permission and shopping phases at le undertaker, the very terrestrial matter of payment enters the picture. We used our Nordstrom Visa to ante up the thousands due. Getting Nordstrom shopping points for charging a funeral must violate some rule of etiquette. We had somehow missed the Emily Post discussions on credit cards, propriety, and funeral arrangements. The nasty business of a funeral tab does crop up during existential thoughts and moments. Still, it astonished me just how much the mundane does make its way into the divine. There is healing power in noticing the mundane when you are aiming for celestial. As we chose a casket, vault, and program and charged it all in one fell swoop, the mundane emerged as a salve for grief. It was a good thing that we didn't have a preset limit on the Nordstrom card. Death carries a hefty tab.

This tandem running of silly details with celestial became one of my most welcome distractions. When the black-suited funeral director returned from running the credit card the mundane crept in again when he asked, "Would you like your receipt with you?" He asked as if we were in Macy's and I had just purchased flatware: "Do you want your receipt with you or in the bag?" My mind, through force of habit, had a moment's respite because this thought bolted through: "No, put it in the bag, vault, whatever."

A sense of humor had seen me through nearly twenty years of Claire's illnesses, hospitalizations, and ongoing uncertainty about her well-being. What saw me through all of that was still available to me. The same things that bring us through any other trial in life can be used for grief. During one of Claire's illnesses, when she was surviving because a machine was breathing for her, I spent every minute with her at the children's hospital. I passed the long hours with observations, curiosity, and temptations. At that time, the hospital had a very odd way of keeping track of costs, a system that would make an internal auditor fly twice backward around his cage. The nurses and doctors removed sticky bar-code tabs from syringes, medicines, and IVs, and simply stuck them on a paper hung on each patient's door. As schedules allowed, the office bean counters would come along and take the filled sheets, replace them with blank sheets, and then go back to the office to add all the sticky code prices to our tab.

One night, during that challenging graveyard (ah!) shift, I had to fight a very strong temptation to lift a few of the sticky bar codes from Claire's chart on the door and spread them around the pod a bit to the other less costly patients. Just the thought of the havoc I could wreak brought a smile during a rough night. Claire was no longer with me here on earth, but why change how we had worked together now? That small moment of humor in the hospital got me through a rugged and risky night. The parable of the bar codes was the same as the small receipt moment at the undertaker's den, or whatever they call it. Dry wit had served us well in the past and would see me through what hurts us the most in life: death.

I also knew from that point forward that my solace would come through observations and insights about what remains largely unspoken. How many times have you heard anyone speak of Visa charges at the funeral home? Not once in my fifty-eight years had someone broached the subject.

Now, as I think back on that gut-wrenching time at the funeral home, I realize that I needed someone like Dot, the mother of five hooligans in the Coen brothers' classic, *Raising Arizona*. In advising the clueless Ed (a.k.a. Holly Hunter), she was pricelessly, persistently, and mercilessly honest: "You got to get him his dip/tet. Do you have a college fund? Who's his pediatrician?" Ed and Hy (Nicholas Cage) were in over their heads trying to care for a child they had stolen and didn't know the first thing about where to go, what to do, and even what to ask. No subject was off limits for Dot. No issue was too sensitive to bring up when it came to the best interests of children or adults.

At that funeral home, I needed a whirling dervish of a busybody who knew about funerals and death to guide me through the elements of undertaking, the physical pain of the loss of one so close, and painstakingly slow process of grief. I never found Dot. But I have become her. Think of me as your Dot for grief. I have matter-of-fact advice and stories for those who have lost a loved one. My journey from nonfunctioning, overpowering grief to a changed soul was remarkable. Better yet, that journey can be taken by anyone—this is the guide for taking grief from its debilitation stage to its final stage of transformation. 'Tis not an easy journey, nor a short one. Slow, deliberate steps through time spent in silent pondering accomplish that transformation. Oh, and you can do it all without the cemetery. Some of us, like me, need a frying pan to the head to understand what we need to do. I'd be willing to bet you can do it on more of a block-plan arrangement and certainly in less than 365 days.[104]

ABOUT THE AUTHOR

Professor Marianne Jennings is an emeritus professor of legal and ethical studies in business from the W. P. Carey School of Business at Arizona State University, having retired in 2011 after thirty-five years of teaching there. She continues to teach graduate courses in business ethics at colleges around the country.

During her tenure at ASU, she served in many different capacities: director of the Joan and David Lincoln Center for Applied Ethics (1995–1999); faculty director for the MBA Executive Program (2006–2007); associate dean (1986–1987); chair of the University Hearing Board (1995–2011); and faculty athletic representative to the NCAA and PAC-10 (1986–1987).

Professor Jennings earned her undergraduate degree in finance and her J. D. from Brigham Young University. Her internships were with the Federal Public Defender and US Attorney in Nevada, and she has done consulting work for law firms, businesses, and professional groups including AES, Boeing, Dial Corporation, Mattel, Motorola, CFA Institute, Southern California Edison, the Arizona Auditor General, the cities of Phoenix, Mesa, and Tucson, the Institute of Internal Auditors, Coca-Cola, DuPont, Blue Cross Blue Shield, Motorola, Mattel, Pepsi, Hy-Vee Foods, IBM, Bell Helicopter, Amgen, Raytheon, and VIAD.

Professor Jennings has authored hundreds of articles in academic, professional, and trade journals. Currently she has six textbooks and monographs in circulation. The seventh edition of her textbook *Case Studies in Business Ethics* and the ninth edition of her textbook *Business: Its Legal, Ethical and Global Environment* were published in January 2011. Her first textbook, *Real Estate Law,* will have its tenth edition published in January

2013. She was added as a coauthor to *Anderson's Business Law and the Legal Environment* in 1997, a text whose twenty-second edition will be published in January 2013. Her book *Business Strategy for the Political Arena* was selected in 1985 by *Library Journal* as one of its recommended books in business/government relations. *A Business Tale: A Story of Ethics, Choices, Success, and a Very Large Rabbit*, a fable about business ethics, was chosen by *Library Journal* in 2004 as its business book of the year. *A Business Tale* was also a finalist for two other literary awards for 2004. In 2000 her book on corporate governance was published by the New York Times MBA Pocket Series. Professor Jennings's book on long-term success, *Building a Business Through Good Times and Bad: Lessons from Fifteen Companies, Each with a Century of Dividends*, was published in October 2002 and has been used by Booz Allen Hamilton for its work on business longevity. Her book on ethical cultures in organizations, *The Seven Signs of Ethical Collapse*, was published by St. Martin's Press in July 2006. Her books have been translated into five languages.

Her columns have been syndicated around the country, and her work has appeared in the *Wall Street Journal, Chicago Tribune, New York Times, Washington Post*, and *Reader's Digest*. A collection of her essays, *Nobody Fixes Real Carrot Sticks Anymore*, first published in 1994, is still being published. She was given an Arizona Press Club award in 1994 for her work as a feature columnist. She has been a commentator on business issues on *All Things Considered* for National Public Radio.

She has conducted more than five hundred workshops and seminars in the areas of business, personal, government, legal, academic, and professional ethics. She has been named professor of the year in the W.P. Carey School of Business in 1981, 1987, 2000, and 2010 and was the recipient of a Burlington Northern teaching excellence award in 1985. In 1999 she was given best article awards by the Academy of Legal Studies in Business and the Association of Government Accountants. She was given best article awards by the Institute of Internal Auditors and Association of Government Accountants in 2001 and 2004. She was a Dean's Council of 100 Distinguished Scholars from 1995 to 2011. In 2000 the Association of Government Accountants inducted her into its Speakers Hall of Fame. In 2005 she was named an All-Star Speaker by the Institute of Internal Auditors. In 2006 her article "Ethics and Investment Management: True

Reform" was selected by the United Kingdom's *Emerald Management Review* from fifteen thousand articles in four hundred journals as one of the top fifty articles in 2005. She was named one of the Top 100 Thought Leaders by Trust Across America in 2010.

She is a contributing editor for the *Real Estate Law Journal, New Perspectives*, the *Smart Manager*, and *Corporate Finance Review*. She was appointed to the Board of Editors for the *Financial Analysts Journal* in 2007. She served as editor-in-chief of the *Journal of Legal Studies Education* from 2003 to 2004. During 1984–1985, she served as then-Governor Bruce Babbitt's appointee to the Arizona Corporation Commission. In 1999 she was appointed by Governor Jane Dee Hull to the Arizona Commission on Character. From 1986 to 1987, she served as ASU's faculty athletic representative to the NCAA and PAC-10. From 1999 to 2009 she served as president of the Arizona Association of Scholars.

She is a member of twelve professional organizations, including the State Bar of Arizona, and she has served on four boards of directors, including Arizona Public Service (now Pinnacle West Capital) (1987–2000), Zealous Capital Corporation, and the Center for Children with Chronic Illness and Disability at the University of Minnesota. She served as chair of the Bonneville International Advisory Board for KHTC/KIDR from 1994 to 1997 and was a weekly commentator on KGLE during 1998. She was appointed to the board of advisers for the Institute of Nuclear Power Operators in 2004. She has appeared on CNBC, *CBS This Morning*, the *Today* show, and *CBS Evening News*.

Personal: Married since 1976 to Terry H. Jennings, Maricopa County Attorney's Office deputy county attorney; five children: Sarah, Sam, and John, and the late Claire and Hannah Jennings.

ENDNOTES

1. Wife, mother, professor, author, lecturer, attorney, and institute instructor.
2. Kevin R. Kosar, "The Two Mrs. Wilsons," *Weekly Standard,* May 9, 2011, 39–40.
3. "On Life and Loss," *Time,* August 20, 2007, 46.
4. *Conference Report*, Apr. 1993, 72; or *Ensign,* May 1993, 54.
5. C. S. Lewis, *A Grief Observed* (San Francisco: Harper, 1961), 33.
6. "O My Father," *Hymns*, 292.
7. Job 6:2.
8. Orson F. Whitney, *The Life of Heber C. Kimball*, (2009), 446, 449–50.
9. Jacob 5:14.
10. Jacob 5:41.
11. Dallin H. Oaks, "Our Strengths Can Become Our Downfalls," Address at Brigham Young University, June 7, 1992.
12. Marion G. Romney, "Satan, the Great Deceiver," given as a conference talk in April 1971, and republished as "Satan, the Great Deceiver," *Ensign,* February 2005.
13. 2 Nephi 26:22, "…he leadeth them by the neck with a flaxen cord, until he bindeth them with his strong cords forever."
14. Matthew 7:3, "And why beholdest thou the mote that is in thy brother's eye, but considerest not the beam that is in thine own eye." *See also* Luke 6:41, 3 Nephi 14:3–5, and Doctrine and Covenants 29:25.
15. *Deseret News, Semi-Weekly,* February 15, 1882, 1.
16. *Teachings of Gordon B. Hinckley* (Salt Lake City: Deseret, 1997), 250.
17. Bruce R. McConkie, *Mormon Doctrine* (1979) 455–56.
18. David McCullough, *John Adams* (New York: Simon & Schuster, 2001), 625.
19. "Behold, I would exhort you that when ye shall read these things, if it be wisdom in God that ye should read them, that ye would remember how merciful the Lord hath been unto the children of men, from the creation of Adam even down until the time that ye shall receive these things, and ponder it in your hearts." Moroni 10:3.
20. Gene R. Cook, "Moroni's Promise," *Ensign,* April 1994.

21. For those who may not understand this reference, some help. There are three Nephites (from the *Book of Mormon* who asked that they not taste death. They asked to be able to roam the earth, helping others, until the time of the Second Coming. Many profess to having seen them. I have not, at least not that I know of. Okay, maybe the unicyclist is a possibility.

22. Joseph Fielding Smith, *Church History and Modern Revelation* (Kila, MT: Kessinger, 2008) 1:253.

23. C. S. Lewis, *A Grief Observed*, 45.

24. Merrill J. Bateman, "A Season for Angels," *Ensign,* December 2007.

25. Proverbs 23:7, "For as he thinketh in his heart, so is he."

26. Jan Underwood Pinborough, "Keeping Mentally Well," *Ensign,* September 1990.

27. Thomas S. Monson, "The Prayer of Faith," *Liahona,* March 1995.

28. "For Times of Trouble," BYU Devotional Address, March 18, 1980.

29. James E. Talmadge, *Articles of Faith,* 12th ed. (Salt Lake City: The Church of Jesus Christ of Latter-day Saints, 1924), 525.

30. C. S. Lewis, *A Grief Observed*, 60.

31. *Ibid.* 62.

32. David Aikman, "Can Civilization Survive without God?" *The American Spectator,* December 2011/January 2012, 33.

33. Ashley Parker, "Children Killed by Mother Are Buried," *New York Times,* April 26, 2011.

34. Only fans of Tom Hanks know where Krakhozia is. In his movie, *The Terminal,* of course.

35. Section 88:121, "Therefore, cease from all your light speeches, from all laughter, from all your lustful desires, from all your pride and light-mindedness, and from all your wicked doings."

36. Proverbs 17:22.

37. Brad Wilcox, "If You Can Laugh At It, You Can Live with It," *Ensign,* March 2000.

38. Jeffrey R. Holland, "This Do in Remembrance of Me," *Ensign*, November 1995.

39. *The Teachings of Spencer W. Kimball,* ed. Edward L. Kimball (Salt Lake City: Bookcraft, 1982), 138.

40. Dallin H. Oaks, "Testimony," *Ensign,* May 2008.

41. "Norman Cousins," *Wikipedia,* http://en.wikipedia.org/wiki/Norman_Cousins.

42. The book was published in 1979. Mr. Cousins also wrote *Human Options: An Autobiographical Notebook* (1980), a book that also explained the role of humor in life. Mr. Cousins's doctors were amazed that he survived for decades longer than they anticipated when he was diagnosed with heart disease.

43. Doctrine and Covenants 1:35, "For I am no respecter of persons, and will that all men shall know that the day speedily cometh; the hour is not yet, but is nigh at hand, when peace shall be taken from the earth, and the devil shall have power over his own dominion." *See also* Acts 10:34, Moroni 8:12, and Doctrine and Covenants 38:16.

44. Some say this is a Hebrew proverb. Others hold that Sir Francis Bacon wrote that a clean body shows reverence to God.

45. Katie Liljenquist, Chen-Bo Zhong, and Adam Galinsky, "The Smell of Virtue: Clean Scents Promote Reciprocity and Charity," *Psychological Science* 21, no. 3 (2010).

46. Genesis 3:19.

47. Doctrine and Covenants 128:7. *See also* Revelation 20:12, 15.

48. Luke 16:3, "No servant can serve two masters: for either he will hate the one, and love the other; or else he will hold to the one, and despise the other. Ye cannot serve God and mammon." *See also* 3 Nephi 13:24, "No man can serve two masters; for either he will hate the one and love the other, or else he will hold to the one and despise the other. Ye cannot serve God and Mammon."

49. Mark 6:22.

50. Matthew 6:21.

51. Doctrine and Covenants 64:10.

52. Jeffrey R. Holland, "The Ministry of Angels," October 2008 conference.

53. Doctrine and Covenants 84:88.

54. 1 Nephi 3:5–6.

55. Part 2, Chapter 22, Paragraph 52.

56. Part 3, Chapter 49.

57. Quoted by Spencer W. Kimball in *Faith Precedes the Miracle* (Salt Lake City: Shadow Mountain, 1972), 38.

58. *Teachings of the Presidents of the Church: Brigham Young* (Salt Lake City: The Church of Jesus Christ of Latter-day Saints, 1997), 262.

59. Mark D. Chamberlain, "The Spiritual Hazards of Fault-Finding," *Ensign,* August 1996.

60. Malachi 4:5–6.

61. Ronald A. Rasband, "The Divine Call of a Missionary," April 2010 Conference, *Ensign,* May 2010.

62. *Ibid.*

63. Doctrine and Covenants 122:7–8.

64. Job 39:19–22.

65. James 1:5.

66. *U..S. News and World Report,* Jan. 22, 1962, p. 90.

67. Matthew 25:1–13.

68. William Grimes, "Barbara Stuart, TV Actress, 81," *New York Times,* May 20, 2011, A19.

69. John Donne, "Devotions upon Emergent Occasions, no. 17 (Meditation)," 1624 (published).

70. This familiar phrase is part of the Anglican burial service and is scripturally grounded, as it were, in Genesis 3:19: "…for dust thou art, and unto dust shalt thou return."

71. Proverbs 15:1.

72. Doctrine and Covenants 121:43.

73. John Lennon wrote the song post-Beatles breakup. It would be his only number one hit of his solo career.

74. "Whatever Gets You thru the Night," *Wikipedia,* http://en.wikipedia.org/wiki/Whatever_Gets_You_thru_the_Night.

75. Genesis 1:3.

76. 2 Nephi 10:14.

77. John 8:12.

78. 3 Nephi 1:15.

79. 3 Nephi 8:20–23.

80. Doctrine and Covenants 50:24.

81. *Hymns,* 1985, 97.

82. Dallin H. Oaks, "Teaching and Learning by the Spirit" *Ensign,* March 1997.

83. John Donne, "Devotions upon Emergent Occasions, no. 17 (Meditation)," 1624 (published).

84. 1 Corinthians 15:55.

85. Dallin H. Oaks, "Teaching and Learning by the Spirit," *Ensign,* March 1997, 11–12, and 14.

86. "Arland D. Williams Jr.," *Wikipedia,* http://en.wikipedia.org/wiki/Arland_D._Williams,_Jr.

87. Richard Rosenblatt, "The Man in the Water," *Time,* January 25, 1982.

88. 1 Samuel 16:7.

89. David Bednar, "Line Upon Line, Precept Upon Precept," BYU Idaho Devotional, September 11, 2001.

90. *Ibid.*

91. Doctrine and Covenants 121:45.

92. Joseph F. Smith, in Conference Report, April 1900, 40.

93. C. S. Lewis, *A Grief Observed,* (San Francisco: Harper), 56.

94. **Robert D. Hales, "Your Sorrow Shall Be Turned to Joy,"** *Ensign,* **November 1983, 66.**

95. James E. Faust, "The Forces That Will Save Us," *Ensign,* January 2007.

96. *Ibid.*

97. "For Times of Trouble," BYU Devotional Address, March 18, 1980.

98. *King Lear*, Act 3, Scene 4, Line 148.

99. 2 Corinthians 4:17.

100. "For Times of Trouble," BYU Devotional Address, March 18, 1980.

101. Kings. 6:16.

102. C. S. Lewis, *A Grief Observed,* 72.

103. C. S. Lewis, *A Grief Observed*, 72.

104. The stories in this book are all true. The names have been changed to protect the privacy of these individuals. They deserve all the best in life for what they did for me, but they may not want the recognition. That's just the type of folks they are. My dear, sweet, and humble cemetery friends – you know who you are.

Made in the USA
San Bernardino, CA
04 August 2014